Hamlyn Colour Guides

Butterflies
and Moths

Hamlyn Colour Guides
Butterflies and Moths

by Ivo Novák

Illustrated
by František Severa

HAMLYN

Translated by Olga Kuthanová
Graphic design by Miloš Lang
Published 1985 by
Hamlyn Publishing,
A division of The Hamlyn Publishing Group Ltd.,
Bridge House, London Road, Twickenham,
Middlesex, England

Printed in Czechoslovakia
ISBN 0 600 30662 3
3/15/16/51-01

CONTENTS

CHARACTERISTICS OF BUTTERFLIES AND MOTHS

Butterflies and moths belong to the largest group of animals, that is the one with the greatest number of species, namely insects. Within this group theirs is the fourth largest order (the Lepidoptera) in terms of species diversity, after the beetles, hymenopterans and dipterans. It is estimated that there are approximately 200 000 species of butterflies and moths on the earth, but only about 120 000 have been described to date. The others are still waiting to be discovered, if that happens at all, for nowadays animals, and that includes butterflies and moths, are declining in number at such a rapid rate that many species may become extinct before they can be discovered.

The development of butterflies and moths is greatest in the tropical regions where they find the most suitable conditions, i. e. a warm climate and ample food for most of the year. The tropics also have the greatest diversity of species. Northward and southward in the temperate zone of both hemispheres the number of species declines with increasing latitude. There are only a few species that are adapted to the harsh conditions of areas beyond the Arctic Circle.

It cannot be said that the lepidopteran fauna of the temperate regions is uninteresting. Although the butterflies and moths there do not attain the large dimensions of their tropical relatives, they are on a par in terms of colourfulness and diversity of shape. Some of the smallest species are of breathtaking beauty, with an assortment of colours and metallic glints and with their wings edged with a delicate fringe, often longer than the breadth of the wing itself. Their way of life is marked by so many peculiarities that it is well worth while trying to learn more about these fascinating creatures. In this book the familiar or in some way interesting species of Europe are illustrated and described with the aim of introducing the representatives of all important families.

Butterflies and moths, being insects (and hence also arthropods), have the basic characteristics of this group. They have a segmented body made up of three distinct parts: the head, thorax and abdomen. The head bears the mouthparts, the antennae, the palps and the eyes. The thorax, made up of three segments, bears three pairs of jointed legs (one pair to each thoracic segment) and also carries two pairs of wings (on the second and third segment). The abdomen is the most greatly segmented of the three body parts; it is made up of ten segments, but only eight are well visible. A typical characteristic of butterflies and moths are the scales covering the entire body of the adults, but mostly the wings; the name Lepidoptera means 'scale wings'. Besides the scales there are numerous hairs on different parts of the body and sometimes on the wings as well. The coloured scales, overlapping each other like the tiles of a roof, form the lovely, elaborate wing patterns; the colours are produced chemically by pigments

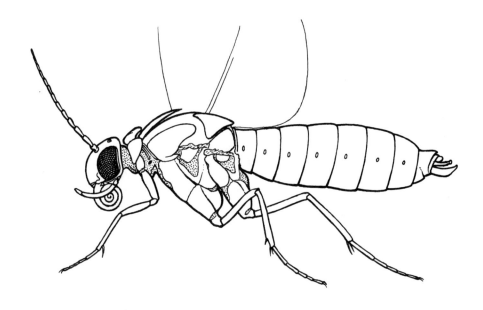

Body of a lepidopterous insect denuded of scales and hairs: head (1 pair of antennae, 1 pair of compound eyes, 1 pair of labial palps); thorax (3 segments, 3 pairs of legs, 2 pairs of wings — merely indicated); abdomen (ventilation openings and external copulatory organs on the terminal segment).

as well as physically by the diffraction and refraction of light. It is very difficult to see the actual skeleton beneath the covering of scales and hairs, and these need to be removed in order to see the individual parts of the skeleton. Such a butterfly or moth that has been 'stripped naked' resembles a child's puppet with movable joints. Like all insects, butterflies and moths breathe by means of tracheae, tubules that convey oxygen to the body tissues.

DEVELOPMENT AND PREIMAGINAL STAGES

For most people the word butterfly or moth evokes the image of the imago or adult. As a rule no thought is given to the complex development that precedes the creature's appearance in its beautifully coloured winged form. In common with all insects butterflies and moths undergo a process known as metamorphosis, in which several completely different growth stages follow in succession — beginning with the egg and ending with the adult. Lepidopterans undergo a complete metamorphosis consisting of four main stages, an active stage always alternating with an immobile or resting stage. The four are: egg, larva or caterpillar, pupa, adult.

7

Egg

The life cycle begins with the egg. The eggs of butterflies and moths are visible with the naked eye; even those of the smallest lepidopterans are relatively large — 0.2–0.3 mm. The largest eggs of robust lepidopterans may be as big as a pea — 3–4 mm. The egg is completely encased in a solid egg shell, or chorion, inside which is the embryo surrounded with a rich supply of yolk, which provides the nourishment for its development. The external surface may be smooth or rough, coarsely sculptured with ridges and hollows or decorated with irregular patches. The shape of the egg exhibits marked diversity and may be spherical, conical, cylindrical, loaf-, bottle- or spindle-shaped, angular or flat and scale-like. The chorion has a minute opening, called the micropyle, through which the mobile sperm can reach the female germ cell in order to fertilize it. If the micropyle is located at the top of the egg, we speak of the egg as being upright; if the micropyle is placed to one side, the egg is described as recumbent.

The females may lay their eggs singly or in characteristic groups: aligned in rows, heaps, a single layer or several layers. Sometimes the females lay the eggs on the surface of leaves or twigs, at other times they carefully insert them into bark fissures, under buds and leaf-sheaths, into rosettes of leaves or in flowers. Newly laid eggs have a soft shell and are usually white or yellowish white but occasionally greenish. The chorion, however, rapidly hardens and the eggs acquire their true colouring, mostly yellow or light green, also grey, brown or even black. The eggs of moths of the genus *Catocala* and those of eggars are brightly coloured. The coloration may sometimes change along with the development of the embryo. The pale eggs may acquire reddish markings; in other cases they may turn a dark colour such as violet or brown. In eggs with a thin, translucent shell the head of the caterpillar is often visible through the chorion towards the end of embryonic development.

Caterpillar

After a certain period, varying greatly according to the species and to external factors, small caterpillars emerge from the eggs. Temperature

Various types of lepidopterous eggs (further types in the pictorial section).

is the most important external factor influencing the development of the egg. The eggs of some species are also affected by insufficient moisture and those of others by excessive moisture. The ideal temperature is around 20 °C. At lower temperatures the development of the embryo slows down or comes to a standstill; at high temperatures (up to a certain limit) it is generally more rapid.

The caterpillar is the stage of activity, feeding and growth. It generally grows quite rapidly. Within two or three weeks, sometimes even sooner, it may become 20 times longer, 2000—3000 times heavier and larger in volume with the head increasing six times in breadth. Not even the most elastic of skins could endure such changes in size, and so the caterpillar moults several times during its development. It casts off the old, tight-fitting skin as well as the head capsule and replaces it with the new, larger and looser skin already developed under the old one. After a few hours the new skin hardens and the caterpillar can again continue feeding. The growth stage between moults is called an instar. Usually there are five or six instars, but sometimes there may be even more. Not all caterpillars, however, grow so rapidly. In some species their development lasts several months, sometimes even years, and there may be a big difference in the length of development even among caterpillars of the same species depending on the seasonal generation to which they belong.

Its rapid growth naturally requires a corresponding amount of food and the caterpillar begins foraging for it as soon as it emerges from the egg. Often the empty chorion serves as the caterpillar's first food so that all traces of its birth are immediately wiped out. For some caterpillars it is essential that the chorion is their first food, and if for some reason they cannot have it they will eat nothing else and so die.

Following its emergence from the egg the caterpillar must seek out the specific food that comprises its diet, be it green leaves, buds, rootlets, bulbs, wood or something else. Some caterpillars gnaw various seeds, apples, nuts, acorns or other fruits. Others feed on matter derived from animals, such as feathers, hairs, beeswax and even the flesh of dead animals. In their natural habitats these caterpillars live in birds' nests and mammals' burrows but when they get into human dwellings and store-houses they can cause considerable damage. There are also predacious caterpillars that either devour their own kind (an example of cannibalism) or other caterpillars and animals.

The great diversity in size, shape and colouring make caterpillars interesting animals. In the smallest moth species the caterpillars are so tiny that they can bore winding tunnels, so-called mines, in leaves by biting out the green tissue between the upper and lower epidermis. Other caterpillars are more than 10 cm long and as thick as the thumb of the hand. Caterpillars may be naked or hairy, spiny or tubercled, smoothly cylindrical or covered with various humps and protrusions. Frequently they have horns and tufts of hair that serve to protect them from their enemies either by making them appear threatening or invisible. Caterpillars have countless enemies, being food for birds as well as other insectivores, so to ensure that at least some survive they have developed a great variety of adaptations serving to make them 'invisible', merging with their environment. Others, when disturbed, suddenly expose parts of their body marked with warning coloration, make use of their chemical weapons, such as foul-smelling or unpalatable secretions, or have poisonous hairs that make life unpleasant for their attackers.

The head of the caterpillar consists of a solid capsule, usually shaped as two incomplete hemispheres. Between these is a triangular forehead and in the front, in the mouth, two powerful, spoon-shaped mandibles. The mouthparts also include, among other things, a silk gland which produces fine silken fibres. Young caterpillars use these fibres to descend from trees or else, like spiders, to be carried by the wind and thus dispersed throughout the countryside. Adult caterpillars use the silk fibres to spin cocoons or to bind together tiny lumps of soil, plant litter and other material when building a chamber in which to pupate. The head also carries the antennae, two pairs of palps and laterally on each side six ocelli (simple eyes as opposed to the compound eyes of the adult insect), usually arranged in a horseshoe pattern.

The body of the caterpillar is composed of 13 segments. Three segments make up the thorax and ten make up the abdomen. Each thoracic segment has a pair of legs consisting of cylindrical or longishconical segments. The abdominal legs, usually located on segments 3—6 and 10, are fleshy and their tips have hard hooks arranged in a circle. A typical characteristic of some families is a reduced number of legs. The caterpillars of some moths are without legs on the third and fourth abdominal segment, and those of geometrid moths have none on the fifth segment as well, thereby leaving them with only two pairs of abdominal legs. Their well-known 'looping' movement is a consequence of this reduction. The caterpillars of prominents have

Various types of caterpillar heads with setae and outgrowths.

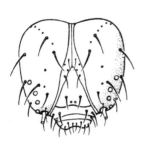 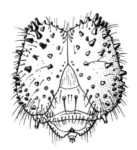 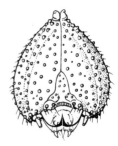

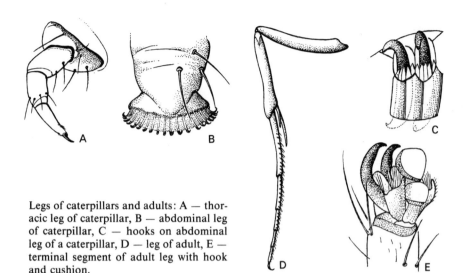

Legs of caterpillars and adults: A — thoracic leg of caterpillar, B — abdominal leg of caterpillar, C — hooks on abdominal leg of a caterpillar, D — leg of adult, E — terminal segment of adult leg with hook and cushion.

the legs on the tenth abdominal segment modified into a fork-like appendage pointing upward from which orange cilia whip out when the caterpillar is disturbed.

Rigid setae cover the caterpillar's body. The location of the setae is quite regular and is often an important feature for the identification of species, aiding experts in distinguishing them from similarly coloured caterpillars. Similar setae are to be found also on the head and extremities. In some species they grow in clusters and form tufts of hair. Hooks and spines on the skin may also be modified into hairs. Otherwise the skin of caterpillars is covered with various tubercles and outgrowths sporting simple as well as branched spines. The location of the outgrowths is characteristic for the given species. Humps are frequently found on the second and third or on the eighth abdominal segment. The caterpillars of hawkmoths are characterized by a peculiar horn on the eighth abdominal segment. The caterpillar of the Tau Emperor (*Aglia tau*) has furcular (forked) appendages on the body when young, but these gradually vanish and there is no trace of them in the fully grown caterpillar. Located on the sides of caterpillars' bodies are ventilation openings (spiracles) through which air enters the tracheae. The tracheae branch and divide into numerous tubules where direct oxygenation of the internal organs takes place. There is one pair of spiracles on the thorax and a further eight pairs on the abdomen.

The caterpillars' way of life shows great variation between species, so does the food they eat, which may be any organic matter. The individual species also differ in the time of their occurrence, the period of

11

Larval (caterpillar) cases of the Coleophoridae and Psychidae families.

development, their daily rhythm and the like. Several species of caterpillars are aquatic. Their adaptation to water may be to such a degree that the breathing organs are modified into branched, protruding gills through which the caterpillar absorbs oxygen direct from the water. Other caterpillars live in cases spun from silk or cemented together from various materials that serve as protection.

Pupa

When fully grown the caterpillar looks about for a safe place to pupate, whereupon it either spins a cocoon or prepares a chamber of sorts and then changes into a pupa. The practically inert pupa does not take food. Inside the rigid case an unusual process then takes place during which the shapeless mass of living matter changes into an adult butterfly or moth. There is no need to describe the pupa here, for the reader will find numerous examples in the illustrated section of this book, but let us merely note that some pupae stand on the hind end and are supported by a silken thread girdling the thorax; others hang by hooks at the tip of the abdomen (the cremaster). Most pupae pass the quiescent period in a recumbent position, either lying freely on the ground or in a cocoon or other hiding place. Such a hiding place may be, for instance, a furled leaf, a hollow inside a stem, a seed capsule, the inside of the fruit of some plant or a tunnel bored in wood. Frequently caterpillars pupate in the ground, where they make a sturdy earthen chamber resembling a hollow mound of soil. After a certain period, the adult butterfly emerges from the pupa.

Adult

The most arresting feature of the adult insect is the colourfulness of the wings. But let us first take a look at the head. Most conspicuous are the large, hemispherical compound eyes (some species also have a pair of small simple eyes, or ocelli, concealed by the fine hairs on the head), large antennae, labial palps and the usually spirally coiled proboscis with which the insect sucks nectar or other juices. In some lepidopterans the proboscis is short, adapted to piercing soft fruits, and in other instances it is reduced altogether, in which case the adults do not take any food, acquiring all the energy they need for their brief life from the fat stored in the body by the caterpillar. The head is joined by a narrow neck to the thorax.

The thorax is composed of three segments. Each bears a pair of legs and the second and third segments both bear a pair of wings. The forewings are larger than the hind wings. Both are reinforced by a complex system of ribs or veins, numbering 15 in all. The various homologous veins have the following specific names: costa, subcosta, radius, media, cubitus, postcubitus and anals. The elaborate wing patterns are formed by minute scales that either contain pigments or produce colours physically by the diffraction or refraction of light, thereby giving the wings their colourful splendour. The characteristic elements of these patterns, certain spots and bands, likewise have specific names, e. g. kidney-shaped spot, wedge-shaped spot, inner and outer cross-band, wavy line.

The legs are composed of ten segments: the coxa, trochanter, femur, tibia, tarsus (5 segments) and the praetarsus. In some lepidopterans (e. g. nymphalids and satyrids) the segments of the forelegs are reduced and the legs are not used for crawling at all.

The abdomen contains the alimentary canal and reproductive organs and its hind end bears the copulatory organs. These external

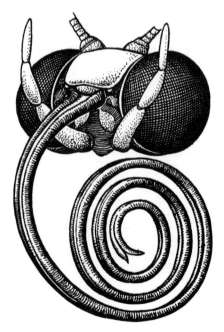

Head of a butterfly with proboscis, compound eyes, labial palps and indication of the antennae.

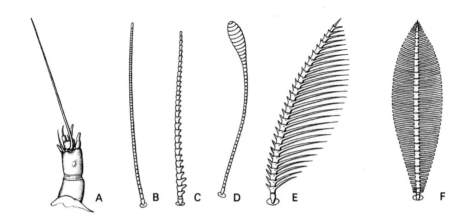

Antennae of caterpillars and adults: A — antenna of caterpillar, B to F — antennae of adults: B — thread-like (filiform), C — saw-toothed (serrate), D — club-shaped (clavate), E — comb-like (pectinate) with branches (rami) on one side, F — comb-like (pectinate) with branches on two sides.

sexual organs are formed from the last two (in the male) or three (in the female) segments and in butterflies and moths (and insects in general) are very distinctive and often an indispensable aid in the exact identification of a species. Examples of the complex structure of these organs are depicted in the pictorial section of this book.

The purpose of the imago is reproduction and its entire life is focused towards this end. The male seeks out a female, copulates with and fertilizes his mate, and the female lays eggs. Thereby ends the life cycle of the butterfly or moth and it dies. The egg marks the beginning of a new cycle.

The butterfly only lives for 3 days.

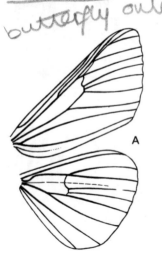

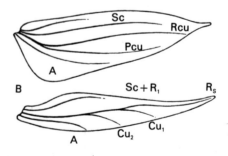

A — complete venation of wing (Noctuidae); B — type with greatly reduced venation (Opostegidae).

DIVERSITY AND VARIABILITY

To describe a species of butterfly or moth in detail and unequivocally is no easy task. Although members of the same species have many characteristics in common, they exhibit variability to a large or small extent in a great many aspects. Individual specimens may differ in size, details of coloration and wing pattern as well as in, for example, behaviour, hardiness and reproductive ability. Variability is a basic characteristic of all living organisms. It enables them to adapt to various external conditions and thus ensures their survival. At the same time it reflects the flexibility of the species, the reaction of a species to the changing conditions of its external environment.

The variability of individuals, populations and species differs in degree. In the case of butterflies and moths the most striking deviations (though not always the most useful) are naturally variations in the coloration and pattern of the wings. The butterfly or moth is said to occur in various forms (the abbreviation for form is f.). In general these are individual forms (also called aberrations) and are not hereditary. Other deviations occur as mutations and are permanent, being passed on to the offspring according to the laws of heredity. Individuals of a single species are sometimes so different that they appear to belong to an entirely different species. Some species, on the other hand, are so variable that it might be rare to encounter two identically coloured individuals.

Another, higher type of variability is geographic variability. If a species is distributed throughout a large area, e. g. all of Europe and Asia, populations in widely distant parts of the range may develop separately, in isolation, in response to the local climate. Isolation is caused by various geographical or geological barriers, such as mountain ranges, large rivers, oceans, deserts, folding of the earth's crust or glaciation. Over a period of tens of thousands of years differences that develop in geographically separated populations may become hereditary in part thus giving rise to various geographic races, termed subspecies (ssp.). A good example of how such subspecies came into being is seen in the Apollo (*Parnassius apollo*), which developed readily distinguishable, geographical races in the separate, isolated mountain ranges of Europe and Asia — several tens have been described in Europe alone.

If such isolation continues for hundreds or thousands of years, the differences among the populations may become so great that they become independent species no longer able to interbreed successfully, accustomed to a different diet, with different life rhythms, etc.

Whereas individual forms are not important from the point of view of systematics, the very opposite is true in the case of geographical forms or races. That is why they are also subject to the rigid rules of nomenclature, i. e. the rules for naming systematic units — species, genera, families, orders, etc.

15

It is necessary to know that the scientific name of a species consists of two names. The first of these names is that of the genus, always written with a capital letter. The second name designates the species and is written with a small initial. This system of two names is called binomial nomenclature. When a third name, designating the subspecies (geographical race), is added it is called trinomial nomenclature. The so-called nominate geographical race is the population of a given territory according to which the species was first described and named, and in its designation the name of the subspecies is identical with that of the species. For example, Carl von Linné described the Swallowtail according to specimens captured in Sweden and so the geographical race inhabiting Sweden is named *Papilio machaon machaon* whereas the slightly different population found in England is named *Papilio machaon britannicus.*

Another kind of variability in butterflies and moths is polymorphism, which presumes the existence of very distinctive groups within the species. This may be sexual, in which case it is termed sexual dimorphism (differences between the male and female), or seasonal, in which case it is called seasonal polymorphism (differences between separate generations in a given year). The term dimorphism is used if it is a case of two different groups and polymorphism in the case of several different groups. In recent years some examples of polymorphism have been given specific names, e. g. differences in coloration alone are designated as dichroism or polychroism.

In many species of butterflies and moths the males differ from the females. In some instances these differences are very slight, e. g. in the pattern, shade of colour, or number of segments in the antennae. In others they are very striking, so much so that the males and females of some species show no resemblance to each other whatsoever. They may differ in coloration (sexual dichroism) or else in size, or in the shape of the antennae, legs or wings. Thus, for example, the male Gypsy Moth (*Lymantria dispar*) is small and brown and his flight is rapid, whereas the female is large, creamy-white and cumbersome in flight. In some geometrids, tussock moths, arctiids and the occasional microlepidopterans the females have degenerate wings and do not fly at all. Male blues are generally blue, while the females are brown. Male emperors have wings with a metallic sheen, whereas in the females this lustrous sheen is absent. The males of many species of moths have pectinate antennae, the females filiform antennae.

Seasonal polymorphism is found in species that have several generations a year. Frequently the individual generations differ in either size or coloration. This is quite common in whites and sulphurs. The second generation of the Scarce Swallowtail (*Iphiclides podalirius*) differs slightly in coloration from the first generation. The reason for these differences, as a rule, is the reaction of insects to the changes in the duration of daylight during the year. A textbook example of seasonal polymorphism, described in the text accompanying the respec-

16

tive colour plate, is illustrated by *Araschnia levana*. Seasonal changes may occur also in the coloration of the caterpillars and pupae. For instance, the summer pupae of the Swallowtail are green, but the winter pupae brown.

SYSTEM OF CLASSIFICATION OF LEPIDOPTERA

It needs no great amount of thought for even the layman to recognize that there are closer ties of kinship between some animals than between others. The same applies to the lepidopterans. In the first place they are readily divided into butterflies and moths. Striking groups are the hawkmoths, burnets and clearwings. More detailed examination and comparison of other characteristics, such as the shape of the wings and antennae, the wing venation, and the mouthparts, enables division into further groups and subgroups.

Whole generations of naturalists have attempted to determine certain principles according to which all living organisms could be categorized in a system. The first to solve this problem with relative success was the famed Swedish scientist Linné. He classified all the plants and animals known to him in his book 'Systema Naturae' which became the basis on which the present classification of organisms has been developed. More than 200 years have passed since the tenth definitive edition was published in 1758. Although much of the original system has been altered as a result of modern research, Linné's underlying principles have remained unchanged. And so to this day butterflies and moths are classified according to the so-called natural system in the animal kingdom (Animalia), phylum of arthropods (Arthropoda), class of insects (Insecta), as the order of butterflies and moths (Lepidoptera).

Within this order they are further divided into families and these in turn into genera. The smallest unit of the system is the species (or subspecies). Auxiliary categories are suborders, superfamilies, subfamilies and other systematic units.

The classification of butterflies and moths is undergoing continual changes, both as a result of comparative morphology and anatomy, palaeontology, genetics and other scientific research, and in accordance with the subjective views of individual naturalists. Originally they were classified according to the morphological characteristics of the adults. In recent years their classification is also taking into account the so-called preimaginal stages, in other words the egg, caterpillar and pupa, and some cytological criteria.

How the concepts of individual authorities differ is best illustrated in terms of the subdivision into families. According to some the Lepidoptera can be divided into 50 families, while according to others there are as many as 120 families. Thus, for example, the nymphalids and satyrids are considered to be two separate families by some authorities and only one by others. The Riodinidae are sometimes considered to be an independent family, and at other times merely a sub-family of the Lycaenidae. Pyralids are sometimes divided into as many as six independent families.

The system currently recognized is that of the Australian scientist I. F. B. Common, which appeared in his book 'The Insects of Australia', and for European butterflies and moths the 1980 classification of the French entomologist P. Leraut, which takes into account the latest findings. According to Leraut the order Lepidoptera is divided into two suborders and 27 superfamilies with their separate families as shown by the following scheme (the less important families have been omitted).

Order: Lepidoptera — Butterflies and Moths
Suborder: Zeugloptera
  Superfamily: Micropterigoidea
    Family: Micropterigidae — Archaic Moths
Suborder: Glossata
  Superfamily: Eriocranioidea
    Family: Eriocraniidae — Primitive Moths
  Superfamily: Hepialoidea
    Family: Hepialidae — Ghost and Swift Moths (Hepialids)
  Superfamily: Nepticuloidea
    Family: Nepticulidae — Nepticulid Moths, Serpentine Miners, Opostegidae
  Superfamily: Tischerioidea
    Family: Tischeriidae
  Superfamily: Incurvarioidea
    Family: Incurvariidae, Adelidae — Longhorns (Fairy Moths)
  Superfamily: Tineoidea
    Family: Tineidae — Tineids, Clothes and Scavenger Moths, Psychidae — Bagworms, Gracillariidae — Narrow-winged Leaf Miners, Blotch Miners
  Superfamily: Yponomeutoidea
    Family: Argyresthiidae, Yponomeutidae — Ermine Moths, Plutellidae
  Superfamily: Gelechioidea
    Family: Coleophoridae — Case Bearers, Oecophoridae, Ethmiidae, Elachistidae, Gelechiidae — Gelechiid Moths
  Superfamily: Sesioidea
    Family: Sesiidae — Clearwings, Choreutidae
  Superfamily: Tortricoidea
    Family: Tortricidae — Leaf Rollers, Tortrix Moths, Cochylidae
  Superfamily: Zygaenoidea
    Family: Heterogynidae, Zygaenidae — Burnets and Foresters
  Superfamily: Alucitoidea
    Family: Alucitidae — Many-plume Moths
  Superfamily: Pterophoroidea
    Family: Pterophoridae — Plume Moths
  Superfamily: Cossoidea
    Family: Cossidae — Goat Moths, Limacodidae — Slug-caterpillar Moths
  Superfamily: Bombycoidea
    Family: Lemoniidae, Lasiocampidae — Eggars, Lappet Moths, Lackey Moths, Endromidae, Sphingidae — Hawkmoths, Saturniidae — Emperor Moths
  Superfamily: Hesperioidea
    Family: Hesperiidae — Skippers
  Superfamily: Papilionoidea
    Family: Papilionidae — Swallowtails and Apollos, Pieridae — Whites and Sulphurs, Lycaenidae, Riodinidae — Metalmarks, Nymphalidae — Nymphalids, Brush-footed Butterflies, Libytheidae — Snout Butterflies, Satyridae — Browns,

Satyrs and Wood Nymphs
Superfamily: Pyraloidea
  Family: Pyralidae — Pyralids
Superfamily: Drepanoidea
  Family: Drepanidae — Hook-tips,
  Thyatiridae
Superfamily: Geometroidea
  Family: Geometridae —
  Geometrids, Inchworms, Loopers
Superfamily: Noctuoidea
  Family: Notodontidae —
  Prominents, Puss Moths,
  Lymantriidae — Tussock Moths,
  Syntomidae — Tiger and Footman
  Moths, Arctiidae, Noctuidae —
  Noctuids, Owlet Moths, Millers
Superfamilies Hesperioidea and
Papilionoidea together form the group of
butterflies generally classed as
Rhopalocera.

ECOLOGY OF BUTTERFLIES AND MOTHS

Butterflies and moths are an inseparable part of nature. They participate in the complex relationships between living and inanimate components and between organisms themselves. They must come to terms with widely varied aspects of inanimate nature, primarily the weather, as well as living nature, i. e. other organisms. On the one hand they are consumers of other organisms, chiefly plants, thereby affecting their life directly or indirectly (by affecting their environment). On the other hand butterflies and moths are themselves food for predacious animals and parasites. They are thus an important link in the food chain and part of the ecosystem of the whole world.

The group of characteristics with which each species is endowed in order to be able to cope with external factors is called its ecological valence. Species with a broad ecological valence stand up well to a wide range of conditions and are flexible. They are able, for example, to live under diverse climatic conditions or feed on a wide variety of foods. A narrow ecological valence, on the other hand, means dependence on a restricted range of conditions and usually also specialization, which may occasionally be quite extreme. Although species with a narrow ecological valence may be adapted to life in very harsh conditions, for instance in high mountains or in the desert, they are incapable of surviving the seemingly mild conditions at lower elevations. Then there is food specialization. Species with a narrow ecological valence are typically monophagous, which means they feed only on a single kind of food, and when this becomes unavailable (e. g. when the plant dies or is destroyed) they are incapable of surviving.

Butterflies and moths thus have diverse requirements and each species must seek a suitable habitat (in the broadest meaning of the term), one that meets its needs and supplies the factors necessary for its existence — this is called an ecological niche. A suitable niche may, for instance be a certain type of stand or plant growth (forest, meadow, waterside thicket), a specific time of the year, a certain phase of the growth of vegetation, a particular quality and chemical composition of the food, a certain temperature and moisture of the immediate environment, the right kind of sunlight, air currents etc.

Some species require a large and complex niche; others are content with one that is small and simple. When a butterfly or moth of a certain species occupies a suitable niche it is averse to sharing it with another species and defends it as best it can. Either it holds its own or is ousted by the intruder. In the latter instance it must find another suitable niche and take it over by displacing the occupant. If there is no suitable niche to be had it must adapt itself to the new conditions and settle for a niche of a different kind. If it is incapable of doing one or the other its fate is death.

The filling of niches of widely varied types and various levels and their mutual interlinking in space, time and so on, give rise to very complex natural communities that maintain their status quo by self-regulation or else change in response to external factors. Nowadays we know that the underlying principle of all these phenomena is the flow of energy. The sun is the ultimate source of the energy necessary for life on our planet. Plants are capable of capturing solar energy and binding it by the synthesis of organic substances. This energy is then passed on to the consumers in the food chain that feed on plants (herbivores). The greater the primary acquisition of solar energy, the greater is the supply for the further links in the ecological chain, thus making life possible for a greater number of species. Where little solar energy is available, the communities have few species and simple interrelations prevail among the organisms. Such communities are easily disrupted and have difficulty recovering from any disturbance. A large supply of energy, on the other hand, allows a much richer community to flourish. For this reason there are only a few species of butterflies and moths in high mountains and in the polar regions; there is not enough energy for many species or for strong interrelations. Warm regions are inhabited by a great abundance of species, their interrelations are more complex and the communities are more resistant to external factors.

Each of the factors of inanimate nature, so-called abiotic factors (temperature, moisture, light), has a separate, individual influence. Of these, temperature is the most important. Butterflies and moths are incapable of regulating their body temperature and can exist only if their body heat is raised to the required level by an outside source. They are thus directly or indirectly dependent on solar radiation or on the temperature of the environment. Their requirements differ. Some species are active at temperatures as low as freezing point or slightly above. The optimum temperature for most species, however, is around 20—25 °C. At higher temperatures their activity increases at first, but then when the temperature nears the limit of endurance it rapidly decreases. Lepidopterans cannot endure being heated above 40 °C for a long time and therefore seek places with a lower temperature, reduce their temperature by fluttering their wings, cool their bodies by sucking liquids and crawl into shady hiding places. Low temperatures are likewise dangerous, particularly when there is a sudden drop. Many species, however, have developed a physiological mechanism that enables them to survive even very severe frosts.

Moisture is another factor important to the life of butterflies and moths. Most of their body tissues are composed of water and this must be replenished continually. Water is important as the basic raw material for the chemical processes within the body, i. e. for the building of body tissues, and as a means of transport for conveying nutrients to all parts of the body and for carrying waste products out of the body. The moisture requirements of the various species differ. Some are very well adapted to life in a dry environment; their bodies are provided with a thick, air-tight cover, hairs prevent evaporation, and they may also be able to take up a large amount of water at one time. The caterpillars obtain the water needed for their life processes from green plants. Other species, or their preimaginal (developmental) stages, cannot survive without a moist environment. The females lay their eggs in places that do not dry out; the caterpillars live inside plants, e. g. inside stems, buds, flowers or fruits, or hide in the ground. Other caterpillars live in cases which besides serving as protection also provide them with increased humidity.

The role of light in the life of butterflies and moths is an interesting one. As a source of energy it is vital to life as such and secondly, it serves as a signal for various life processes. Every year, for millions of years, the hours of daylight have regularly become shorter and longer during the course of the year and the seasons have likewise changed regularly, favourable seasons alternating with ones that are less favourable. And so butterflies and moths learned to use the astronomical clock to their benefit. With the aid of light signals they make timely preparations to survive the inclement seasons and, similarly, they know when it is time to hatch so that there will be enough food for the offspring.

Dormancy is any type or period of inactivity in the development of a butterfly or moth. There are many types of such inactivity and they are very complex. The two basic types are quiescence and diapause, plus many intermediate types. Quiescence is the immediate reaction to a change in external factors: generally a change in temperature, occasionally also humidity. When the temperature or humidity drops below the optimal value, the organism ceases to be active. When suitable conditions are restored, however, it immediately continues growth or reproduction. In substance, quiescence is the ability to become immobile with cold or drought and is not dependent on light.

Diapause is a far more complex type of dormancy. It is a period of inactivity in the course of development triggered off by hormonal changes in the organism long before the onset of an unfavourable season. The length of daylight is the impulse that stimulates the necessary changes in the organism. When the days are short, the physiological processes within the body are different from those that take place when the days are long; the glands produce different substances or may temporarily cease functioning. Thus the lengthening of the hours of daylight in spring awakens the hibernating caterpillar to renewed life, is the impulse for the butterfly or moth to emerge from the cocoon, or the signal for the caterpillar to gnaw its way out of the hibernating egg. A certain length of daylight stimulates the ripening of eggs in the ovaries of the females or sexual activity in the males. It determines whether there will be a further generation the same year, whether the pupa will remain resting for several days or several months, etc. Diapause may occur in any of the developmental stages and the light signal generally precedes the onset of dormancy by quite a long time. This is extremely important for the survival of the species, for the impulse is given at a time when food is plentiful and the caterpillar or imago (i. e. the feeding stages) is able to store sufficient fat to survive the inclement period. The length of daylight may also affect the coloration of the future adult (seasonal polymorphism).

Of the factors of a living nature — so-called biotic factors — the most important is food, which is the principal source of energy. Butterflies and moths, being heterotrophic organisms, are entirely dependent on the food produced by other living organisms, chiefly plants. Plants are fed on by some adults as well as by caterpillars. Only occasionally do caterpillars feed on animals or animal products such as feathers, hairs or dead animal remains.

In terms of food lepidopterans are divided into three main groups: polyphagous, oligophagous and monophagous.

Polyphagous lepidopterans are not particularly choosy and feed on many kinds of food. For the caterpillars of some species the list of plants they do not feed on would be shorter than that of those they do. For instance, the caterpillars of the well known Silver Y Moth (*Autographa gamma*) were found or experimentally reared on more than 200 species of plants belonging to 51 different plant families.

Oligophagous lepidopterans have more specific requirements and feed on only some species of plants belonging to just one family or even to a single genus. At other times the oligophagy is ecologically limited, e. g. the diet consists only of various aquatic plants, various species of tree lichens, plants with hollow stems, plant bulbs or tubers. There is no sharp dividing line between polyphagy and oligophagy.

Most highly specialized are monophagous lepidopterans. These feed on only a single kind of food — on a single species of plant or even a certain part of the plant, e. g. buds, fruits, leaves or only parts of the leaves. Explicit monophagy is relatively rare in butterflies and moths but is typical for certain families, e. g. the Coleophoridae, Sesiidae and Lithocolletidae. Like every specialization, monophagy is double-edged. Although sometimes it enables the species to utilize a supply of food other organisms cannot consume, when its host plant disappears the species disappears (dies out) as well.

ADAPTATION

Most adaptations are a reaction to the pressures of the environment. Resistance to cold and tolerance of a moist or dry environment result from the process of natural selection in response to the external environment. Other adaptations are the characteristic ways by which butterflies and moths defend themselves by attempting to hide from their enemies. Many noctuids and geometrids imitate the background of the plants and objects on which they rest. Many are indistinguishable from, for example, lichens, the bark of trees, rocks or the ground. The caterpillars of geometrids, notodontids, noctuids and other moths look like twigs with buds, bits of twigs, galls or twisted leaves. Frequently butterflies and moths simulate, in shape and coloration, much-feared insects avoided by predators.

REPRODUCTIVE CAPACITY

As in all other insects the reproductive capacity of butterflies and moths is immense. The female generally lays hundreds of eggs, and some species lay batches consisting of several thousand. If all these eggs developed into adults, they would greatly outnumber the parent generation. Where there are two or more generations a year, the number of offspring would run into the millions or even billions. This, of course, would be a catastrophe: with that many caterpillars the countryside would be left without a single green leaf. Although such calamities occur now and then, population explosions generally do not happen for nature has sufficient means to control them.

If a population density similar to that of the parent generation is to be maintained, only two reproductively successful adults may develop from each batch. The rest must die. Thus the total mortality of the offspring comes close to 100 per cent. In the course of natural development individuals are actually exterminated in a drastic way. Unfavourable weather conditions head the list of causes of death: many young caterpillars are washed away or killed by strong rains and some do not survive sudden changes in temperature. Caterpillars are furthermore food for various animals. Birds kill vast numbers, particularly when they are feeding their young. Ground caterpillars fall prey to insectivorous mammals such as moles, shrews and hedgehogs. Certain beasts of prey, such as the fox, badger and bear, consider a plump caterpillar or pupa a tasty morsel. Mice and voles are generally considered pests, but besides plants they also consume a large number of butterfly and moth pupae. Many caterpillars are killed by predacious insects such as ground beetles, or are preyed on by parasites such as the larvae of ichneumons, braconids or larvaevorids. And last of all, like all other animals, butterflies and moths fall prey to various diseases during the course of their development. The eggs may be attacked by fungi or bacteria or the caterpillars killed by viruses, various alimentary diseases or fungi. Pupae also are attacked by fungi and other micro-organisms. As well as birds, bats are among the greatest enemies of adult lepidopterans, chiefly nocturnal moths, which they catch in large numbers.

Occasionally, however, for some reason one or another of the naturally regulating forces fails, and then the mortality of the offspring is reduced. If this persists for several ensuing generations, the result is a population explosion of the species, a so-called gradation. In the first phase the density of the population increases, but then it reaches its peak and begins to decrease. Such a decrease is caused on the one hand by the growth in number of parasites and predators in response to the abundance, and on the other by the death by various diseases to which hungry caterpillars are prone when all the available food has been eaten. After a time everything returns to normal but the vegetation damaged by such a population explosion takes a long time to recover. Where field crops are affected, man himself is a victim as well. Production is endangered, the yield may be lower or the crops may be destroyed completely. Not so long ago (in 1977) in the northern parts of Germany there was an explosion of the Turnip Moth, which destroyed several million hectares of potatoes, sugar beet and vegetables. In the sixties the Silver Y Moth proliferated in like manner, the moth *Charaeas graminis* caused the defoliation of mountain meadow vegetation, and in recent years the Green Oak Tortrix (*Tortrix viridana*) and the Mottled Umber (*Erannis defoliaria*) have often wreaked havoc in oak woods by stripping off the leaves. Fruit trees are prey to outbreaks of the caterpillars of the Winter Moth (*Operophtera brumata*), the Brown-tail Moth *(Euproctis chrysorrhoea)* and the Lackey (*Malacosoma neustria*). Every year damage is done to apples by the caterpillars of the Codling Moth (*Cydia pomonella*). Grape vines, maize and other crops are also damaged by specific lepidopterans. Countless microlepidopterans feed on stored goods, fabrics, etc. Far outnumbering these, however, are the many species that do not cause any damage, are practically unnoticeable and modestly fill some role in nature's complex cycle and many food chains. In addition to this they enrich man's life with their beauty and by contributing towards the balance of nature and thereby a healthy environment.

COLLECTING BUTTERFLIES AND MOTHS

Declining numbers of butterflies and moths in the wild suggest that the days of capturing them freely are gone and making stereotyped collections of large lepidopterans has become an undesirable anachronism. The sheer scarcity of many species has meant that butterflies and moths should be protected rather than collected and should be caught only exceptionally, mainly for study purposes. True nature lovers could study families that have been less thoroughly researched to date, particularly the group of microlepidoptera, imperfectly known species, larval stages (about which relatively little is known), life cycles and items of interest or even complex laws of existence of individual species. A lot of observations can be made without killing the insects and if it is necessary to catch some specimen now and then to examine it in detail, why not release the butterfly after having made the identification? The great advances in the technology of photography offer unprecedented possibilities of 'capturing' butterflies and moths in colour in their natural habitats, on plants and flowers, in motion, as well as engaged in other activities, and thus create inimitable collections that can be used for book illustration as well as for further study.

But first where should one go to see lepidopterans in the wild, and when? Naturalists interested not only in butterflies but also in moths can see some species at almost any time of the year, for certain kinds of moths are still flying in the depths of winter. Late spring and summer is, of course, the time when most butterflies and moths are on the wing in woodlands, meadows and damp valleys with lush vegetation, some species can even be found on mountains, flourishing during the brief flowering season.

Several types of entomological net are available to enable you to catch butterflies. The standard butterfly net has a long, bag-shaped net made of mosquito netting, organdy or some other fine fabric fastened to a metal ring about 30–45 cm (12–18 in) in diameter. The ring is attached to a wooden or metal stick.

Many night-flying moths — particularly geometrids and noctuids — are drawn irresistibly towards light. Ultraviolet rays in particular have an extraordinarily strong effect and thus a far greater number of moths will come to the light of a mercury vapour lamp than to that of an ordinary electric light bulb. The light source is placed in front of a white sheet to increase the effect of the light and soon many moths arrive, flying about in the immediate area, settling on the ground, grass and sheet, or moving about on the sheet.

Equipment for capturing lepidoptera with light at night.

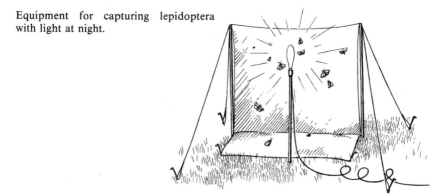

The bait attracts only those lepidopterans that feed. Species with degenerate mouthparts cannot be captured by this means, but it is an excellent method of obtaining numerous types of moths. A sweet-smelling or fermenting liquid is used as bait. Most widely recommended is beer boiled briefly with a little honey, coated onto several apples cut into small pieces. The fruit slices are attached to string and then dipped into this liquid and hung on the branches of trees and shrubs.

Bait is hung up or spread in the evening, for the moths arrive in greatest numbers shortly after dusk.

Virgin lepidopterous females also may be used in an interesting way, for a newly hatched female emits a particular odour which attracts males. This comes from chemical substances called pheromones and enables the sexes to locate one another more readily in the wild. Females to be used as lures are generally reared from caterpillars. At the proper time the virgin female is taken to a place where the species is likely to occur. She is placed in a cage so that the males cannot get to her and fertilize her, for then she would immediately lose the ability to produce the odour of the pheromones and thereby also the power to attract the opposite sex. This method can be used to capture only the species to which the female belongs, for these sexual odours are very specific.

REARING BUTTERFLIES AND MOTHS FROM EGGS, CATERPILLARS AND PUPAE

By rearing butterflies and moths the collector obtains perfect, undamaged specimens and furthermore learns in detail about the life of the respective species, its various requirements in terms of food, temperature, moisture and so on. Caterpillars are interesting, variously coloured and furnished with peculiar outgrowths giving them strange shapes that are intended to resemble various objects. Learning about caterpillars is just as important as learning about adult specimens. Eggs for rearing can be obtained from a female which has hatched from a pupa collected from your own or a friend's garden. Rear them, watching them turn into pupae.

When reared from eggs small caterpillars will emerge after several days or weeks. These are kept in small containers at first, later in larger receptacles of glass or plexite or large breeding cages with sides of fine mesh wire netting. When rearing caterpillars it is necessary to supply fresh food almost daily, to remove the excrement, which soon becomes mouldy and may be a source of infection, and to maintain adequate humidity (neither too low nor too high) and the correct temperature inside the cage. At a low temperature (10 ° to 15 °C) the development of the caterpillars takes a very long time. Extremely high temperatures (above 25 °C) and high humidity accelerate development but increase the danger of infection, which means almost certain death for the caterpillars and a waste of all the collector's care and effort of often several weeks' duration. Exposure to direct sunlight is likewise detrimental, particularly if the caterpillars are kept in air-tight receptacles, for example of glass.

When the end of the caterpillars' development draws near, it is necessary to provide the right conditions for pupation. Some caterpillars spin a cocoon in a corner of the breeding cage, others require a layer of earth in which to make a cell for pupation, and still others need sawdust, soft tissue paper (e. g. Kleenex) or other materials to build a suitable cocoon.

Pupae do not require special care. All they need is to be sprinkled now and then with water and to be left in natural conditions for at least a few weeks in winter. They should never be taken out of the webs of cocoons, which provide them with the best microclimate.

The collector's reward for all his efforts will be a perfect adult specimen, often with its virgin coloration, which in natural conditions disappears after the first brief flight. For example, the Narrow-bordered Bee Hawkmoth (*Hemaris tityus*) and the Broad-bordered Bee Hawkmoth (*H. fuciformis*), when they emerge, have the translucent areas of the wings covered with scales.

PROTECTING BUTTERFLIES AND MOTHS

In the past few decades butterflies and moths have declined markedly in number, particularly in industrially and agriculturally developed nations. This is best demonstrated by the butterflies. In areas where intensive farming is practised one will nowadays see only an occasional white, and flowering fields of clover with nymphalids, sulphurs and swallowtails flitting about are long since a thing of the past.

It is estimated that in as late as the 1940s some 45 species of field and meadow butterflies and 25 woodland species still occurred in abundance in central Europe. Nowadays only 10 or 11 species may be said to be plentiful in meadows, and approximately 9 species in forests. And even these are declining in numbers. Practically all the other species have become what is termed 'rare'. Only very few have adapted to cultivated countryside. The greatest damage has been caused by the ill-considered use of chemical agents to protect plants. Unfortunately, when spraying or dusting fields to eradicate a mass occurrence of some destructive agricultural pest, forests may be affected as well. Frequently the fine powder or poisonous mist falls not only on cropland but is also carried elsewhere. Nowadays on flowering hillsides and in flowering hedgerows there is no sign of the burnets, fritillaries and satyrids that used to rest on Field Scabious and Wild Thyme. The number of moths and microlepidopterans has also declined.

The diminishing number of classic meadows and the drainage of damp meadows has had an unfavourable effect on the life of insects. There are increasingly fewer flowers on heavily fertilized, recultivated meadows and hence also less food for butterflies and moths. Another catastrophe for lepidopterans is the annual burning of old grass in spring, for the eggs, caterpillars and pupae of butterflies and moths as well as useful other insects overwintering there are destroyed with the grass.

In the case of many species the principal reason for the decline in their numbers is their inability to adapt to the drastic changes being made in their environment. Man often destroys whole biotopes and alters the countryside in such a way as to make it unsuitable. Some species are exterminated by these changes indirectly, by the disappearance of their food plants.

Many nations throughout the world and especially in Europe now have so-called Red Books of endangered species — not just butterflies and moths but other animals as well. Rare species are protected by law. Conservation-minded citizens are becoming more vocal in their justified protest against the catching of butterflies and moths merely as mementoes or for purely commercial reasons. Some interest groups and conservation organizations are even attempting to breed butterflies and moths in captivity. This would satisfy the market demand for certain large species and prevent their being collected in the wild. The release of individuals reared in captivity, their return to the wild, might also strengthen endangered natural populations.

It is man's obligation to preserve on this planet the greatest possible wealth of plant and animal species. In their way they are historical monuments created by nature over millions of years. It would be a sad thing if, in the case of such beautiful creatures as butterflies and moths, we had to ask ourselves the question: will they survive the year 2000?

COLOUR ILLUSTRATIONS

Swallowtail
Papilio machaon L.

Papilionidae

The family of swallowtails and apollos is not a large one. It comprises some 700 species distributed throughout the world, mostly in the tropics. However, it includes among its members the largest butterflies in the world, members of the genus *Ornithoptera* which are becoming increasingly rare. Europe is the home of ten species of swallowtails that are beautifully coloured but nowhere near the size of their tropical relatives. One of the loveliest is the illustrated Swallowtail, which lives not only in Europe but also in northern Africa, the temperate regions of Asia to Japan and in North America. Throughout this extensive range it occurs as several geographic races differing in size and in the coloration of certain parts of the wing. Otherwise there is not much variability in the wing pattern, and the male and female differ only in size, not in colouring. The pupae are of interest as there are two differently coloured types. Summer pupae, which may be found in June and July, are a dingy green, while winter pupae are brown. The adult butterflies emerge from the first (green) pupae after a short time, whereas the brown pupae hibernate.

Over the last few decades the Swallowtail has become nearly extinct and in many countries is protected by law. Its disappearance has been caused by changes in the methods of farming, i. e. the use of fertilizers, pesticides, and the ploughing up of meadows for crop cultivation or their use as pastureland for intensive grazing.

The Swallowtail (1) has a wingspan of 50—75 mm; the female is slightly larger than the male. The colourful caterpillar (2) feeds on umbelliferous plants (carrot, fennel, caraway). The pupa (3) hibernates. The butterfly inhabits meadowland biotopes from lowlands to mountains up to about 2000 m. The number of generations produced in a year depends on the climate and altitude: in colder districts there is only one, but in warmer districts there are two or three. The butterflies are on the wing from April till June and from July till August.

The Scarce Swallowtail (*Iphiclides podalirius* L.) (4) has a wingspan of 50—70 mm. Apart from their difference in size the male and female are alike. This butterfly is more thermophilous (warmth-loving) than the afore-mentioned species and is found in forest-steppe. In central Europe there are two generations a year, and in the south three. The butterfly is on the wing from

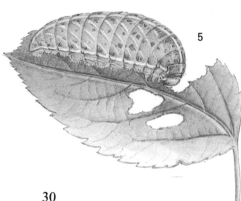

5

April till June and in late summer from
August to September. The caterpillar (5)
feeds on Blackthorn, apple, hawthorn
and the like. The pupa hibernates. This
butterfly is protected by law in some
countries for it is rapidly declining in
number.

Southern Festoon
Zerynthia polyxena D. et Sch.

One would not think that this strikingly coloured, thermophilous butterfly, reminiscent of the magnificent species of the tropics, is a native of Europe. The species was described according to the population in the vicinity of Vienna. The centre of its distribution, however, is in the southern and eastern Mediterranean region, extending east as far as Asia Minor. Some 20 geographical forms have been described throughout its range, the best known being ssp. *cassandra* Hb. found in southwestern Europe. The Southern Festoon occurs in lowland districts. Early in spring it is on the wing in steppes and forest-steppes, by the waterside, on embankments, dikes and around vineyards, in other words wherever its food plants — various species of birthwort — grow. Its flight is fluttering and close to the ground and it is not wary. It is one of nature's spring gems and in many countries is protected by law from indiscriminate insect collectors and dealers. In recent years its numbers have been declining and in some localities the species is becoming rare. However, greater damage than collecting is caused by the pesticides used to protect agricultural crops and by the burning in spring of dry grass and plants in which the pupae hibernate.

Also found in Europe is the species *Z. rumina* L., which occurs in northern Africa and the western Mediterranean region. Another similar species is *Allancastria cerisii* Godt., found in southeastern Europe and Asia, a range it shares with the Southern Festoon.

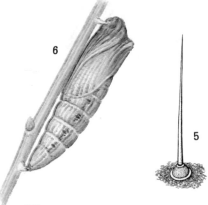

6

5

The Southern Festoon (1, 2) has a wingspan of 45—55 mm; the female is slightly larger than the male. There is one generation a year and the butterflies are on the wing in spring — from April till June. The development of the caterpillars (3) lasts from May till July, when they may be found, often in large groups, on various species of birthwort. They are brightly coloured: yellow-orange with red

and black tubercles (4), each covered
with numerous bristles (5) growing from
a small wart at the base. The caterpillars
smell strongly of the plant they feed on,
which evidently serves to protect them
effectively against enemies. The pupae (6)
are attached front end upwards to plant
stems, staying like this on the dry plant
litter from summer until the following
spring.

33

Apollo
Parnassius apollo L.

Papilionidae

Its beauty has made the Apollo one of the most popular of butterflies. Such popularity has its drawbacks, however, for the Apollo is widely hunted by man as a profitable commercial item and in many places has become extinct or extremely rare. It is one of the few butterflies to be placed on the world list (the Red Book) of endangered species. It is distributed intermittently in mountain and hilly districts from western Europe to central Asia. Similar species are to be found in eastern Asia. The Apollo is not a typical mountain species, even though in the Alps it occurs at altitudes up to 2500 m. Some sites are located (or rather were recorded in the past) at an elevation of 200 m. Isolated populations in the Pyrenees, Alps, Apennines, the Balkans, Carpathians and northern Europe developed into separate geographic races. This species even tends to have local forms in separate large valleys.

Found at high altitudes in the Alps is the similar Small Apollo (*Parnassius phoebus* F.). It occurs in fewer places but its distribution extends farther east than does the Apollo's. It is also found in North America.

4

The Apollo has a wingspan of 65—75 mm. The female is slightly larger than the male (1), darker coloured and with brighter red 'eyes' on the wings. There is only one generation a year. Adult butterflies may be seen from May (in southern Europe) till August (in the north and at higher elevations). The eggs usually hibernate, although if the weather in autumn is warm the caterpillars may emerge then. The caterpillars, coloured black with red-orange markings (2), feed on various kinds of stonecrops and houseleeks (White Stonecrop, Orpine,

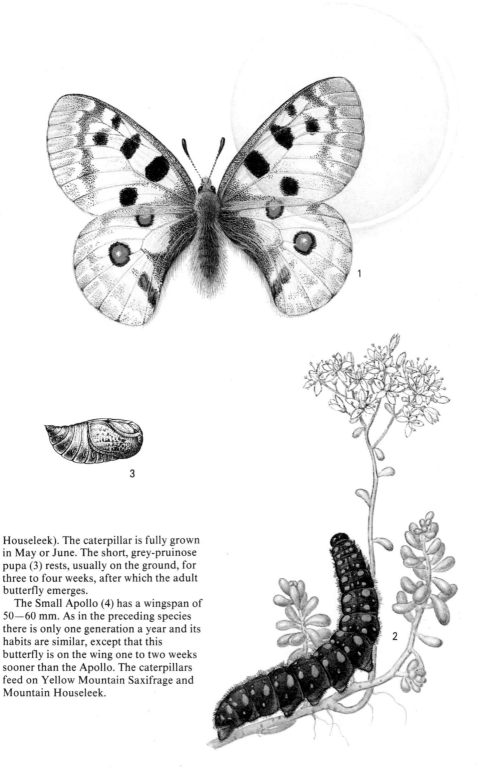

Houseleek). The caterpillar is fully grown in May or June. The short, grey-pruinose pupa (3) rests, usually on the ground, for three to four weeks, after which the adult butterfly emerges.

The Small Apollo (4) has a wingspan of 50—60 mm. As in the preceding species there is only one generation a year and its habits are similar, except that this butterfly is on the wing one to two weeks sooner than the Apollo. The caterpillars feed on Yellow Mountain Saxifrage and Mountain Houseleek.

Large (Cabbage) White
Pieris brassicae L.

The family Pieridae comprises two markedly different groups of butterflies: the whites and the sulphurs. It includes approximately 2500 known species, of which 45 are native to Europe. The Large (Cabbage) White is one of the most abundant butterflies in Europe. It thrives wherever vegetables are grown. In the wild the caterpillars feed on various cruciferous plants but in horticultural areas they are occasionally serious pests. This species is also distributed in northern Africa and eastwards to the Himalayas. It is absent only from the colder regions of northern Europe. When there is a great upsurge in their number the butterflies make invading migrations in quest of new sources of food. These, however, are not regular migrations such as are undertaken by other butterflies.

The following two whites are likewise very abundant species even in cultivated countryside. The Small White (*P. rapae* L.) has been introduced to all parts of the world and, like the Large (Cabbage) White, is a considerable pest in fields and gardens where vegetables are grown. However, it feeds on a wider variety of plants, including reseda, nasturtium, etc. The Green-veined White (*P. napi* L.) is generally distributed in the wild throughout the entire Palaearctic region, i. e. from northern Africa through Europe and Asia to Japan, and is also found in North America. It is one of the first spring butterflies.

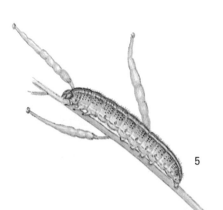

The Large (Cabbage) White has a wingspan of 50—65 mm. The male differs from the female (1) by having the wings devoid of black spots in the centre. There are generally two generations a year — sometimes also a partial third — which are on the wing from April till early June, then again from July till August, and sometimes also in September and October. The caterpillars (2) may be found from June till September on cruciferous plants. The pupae (3) hibernate.

The Small White (4) has a wingspan of 40—50 mm. The male differs from the female in the same way as do the preceding as well as the following species. There are two to three overlapping generations that are on the wing from March till September. The caterpillar (5) may likewise be found

5

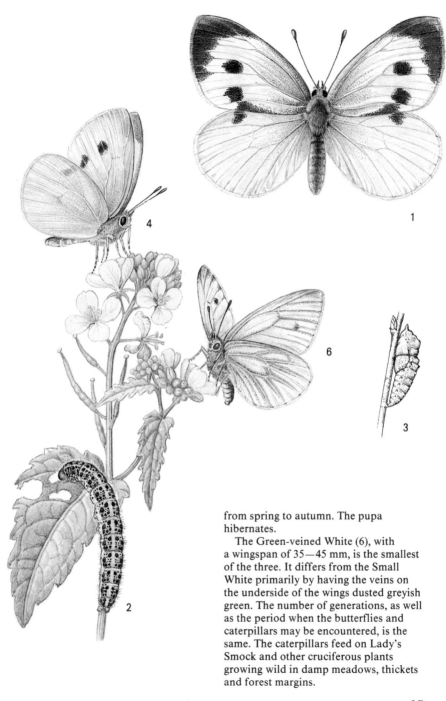

from spring to autumn. The pupa hibernates.

The Green-veined White (6), with a wingspan of 35—45 mm, is the smallest of the three. It differs from the Small White primarily by having the veins on the underside of the wings dusted greyish green. The number of generations, as well as the period when the butterflies and caterpillars may be encountered, is the same. The caterpillars feed on Lady's Smock and other cruciferous plants growing wild in damp meadows, thickets and forest margins.

Black-veined White
Pieridae
Aporia crataegi L.

With its white, translucent, black-veined wings this large butterfly resembles a small Apollo. Its anatomical features, vein pattern, type of caterpillar and pupa, however, clearly indicate it belongs to the whites, to a separate genus with a single species native to Europe. In the case of this butterfly it is the small caterpillars that hibernate among leaves in silken nests resembling those of the Brown-tail Moth; such 'nests' are unusual for butterflies. The Black-veined White is widespread in the warm regions of Europe, in northern Africa, and in the temperate regions of Asia to the Far East. It is a migratory butterfly. The caterpillars feed on fruit trees and were formerly great pests of fruit orchards. In the present century, however, this species has become extinct in many places and its occurrence in harmful numbers is relatively rare, particularly in central Europe.

The Orange Tip (*Anthocharis cardamines* L.), another white, is also a European butterfly of note. It is distributed throughout the Palaearctic region to Japan. The male, with a striking orange patch on each forewing, brightens our meadows, thin broad-leaved woods and gardens in springtime. Its numbers also, alas, have registered a marked decline in the past decades.

The Black-veined White (1) has a wingspan of 50—65 mm. The male and female are more or less alike. There is only one generation a year, which is on the wing from May till July. The caterpillars (2) feed on the leaves of cultivated fruit trees (apricot, pear, apple, cherry, etc.) and wild shrubs of the rose family, chiefly Blackthorn and hawthorn. The young caterpillars hibernate and complete their development in May. The pupal stage (3) lasts no more than two to five weeks.

The Orange Tip has a wingspan of 35—45 mm. The male (4) differs from the female (5) by having an orange patch on the upperside of each forewing. This species can be identified from other whites by the colourful underside of its hind wings. The butterflies are on the wing from April till June; in mountain districts where spring comes later they may be seen even in July. The caterpillars feed from May till August on cruciferous plants, such as *Alliaria* and *Cardamine*. The pupa (6), which has a very characteristic shape, hibernates.

Pale Clouded Yellow
Colias hyale L.

Pieridae

The Pale Clouded Yellow is one of the commonest species of sulphurs. It occurs in large numbers in farm country but prefers dry meadows, fallow land and forest-steppes. It is distributed throughout the warmer regions of Europe and in Asia to the Altai Mountains. A good flier, it occasionally appears in districts where it does not normally occur, chiefly high up in the mountains or in northern Europe. The New Clouded Yellow (*Colias australis* Verity) is a very similar but more warmth-loving species which prefers biotopes of a definitely steppe or forest-steppe character. The two species differ slightly in the shape of the wings and the black markings but can be distinguished more readily by the coloration of the caterpillars and by the plants they feed on. It was not until the beginning of the twentieth century that it was discovered that they were two separate species.

The Clouded Yellow (*Colias crocea* Fourcr.) is one of the orange-coloured sulphurs. It is a migrant. In favourable years it spreads throughout Europe, where it may remain even for several years, but it resides permanently only in warmer regions, chiefly the parts of Europe and Africa bordering the Mediterranean and in Asia all the way to Afghanistan. It may be found in fields and meadows, often even in mountains. Some years it is plentiful, but then it may not put in an appearance for some time. The female differs from the male by having yellow spots scattered in the black border.

4

The Pale Clouded Yellow has a wingspan of 40—45 mm. The male (1) is yellow, the female whitish. There are two or three generations a year, which are on the wing in April and May, July and August, and September and October. The caterpillar (2) hibernates. The pupal stage (3) lasts only a matter of days. The caterpillar feeds primarily on Lucerne, also on coronilla and other leguminous plants.

The Clouded Yellow (4) has a wingspan of 35—50 mm. Females,

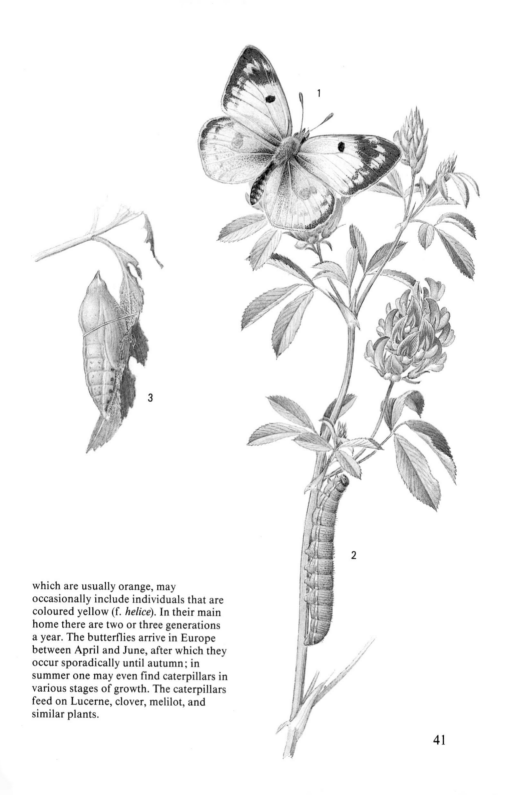

which are usually orange, may
occasionally include individuals that are
coloured yellow (f. *helice*). In their main
home there are two or three generations
a year. The butterflies arrive in Europe
between April and June, after which they
occur sporadically until autumn; in
summer one may even find caterpillars in
various stages of growth. The caterpillars
feed on Lucerne, clover, melilot, and
similar plants.

Moorland Clouded Yellow
Colias palaeno L.

Pieridae

The Moorland Clouded Yellow inhabits a vast territory in the northern Palaearctic, from Europe to Japan. Its distribution also extends to North America, where it occurs in Alaska and northern Canada. In tundra it has a continuous distribution; further south it has a disrupted range, being restricted to places with a climate congenial to the life of this butterfly, i. e. higher up in the mountains or on moors. The occurrence of the species is furthermore dependent on the presence of the one plant it is known to feed on — the Bog Bilberry. It belongs to the group of so-called boreo-alpine species which have a continuous distribution in the north but a disrupted range, usually restricted to the mountains, in the south. In central Europe it is a relict of the Ice Age. The insular distribution of the separate populations brings with it the formation of different geographic races. Linné described the butterfly found in Sweden, the so-called nominate form — ssp. *palaeno* L. The Alps are the home of a smaller race, ssp. *europomene* O., and the moors of central Europe are the home of ssp. *europome* Esp. The Moorland Clouded Yellow is relatively common in suitable biotopes, but when these environments are destroyed it disappears. This has been the case in recent years because of the increase in peat mining. The Moorland Clouded Yellow can survive only in those places where its habitat is preserved, chiefly in natural reserves. On moors earmarked for peat mining its fate is indelibly sealed. It is a lovely butterfly that deserves the protection of strong conservation measures.

5

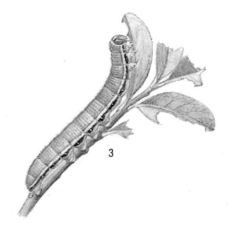

3

The Moorland Clouded Yellow has a wingspan of 40—50 mm. It exhibits marked sexual dimorphism and dichroism: the male (1) is bright yellow with a sharply defined black border, while the female is whitish with a blurred border. In a state of arousal the female (2) raises her abdomen. Occasionally one may encounter a yellow female — a form described as *illgneri*. There is one

generation a year, and it is on the wing in June and July. The caterpillar (3), coloured green with yellow, black-edged stripes on the sides of the body, feeds on the Bog Bilberry. It hibernates and in May changes into a green pupa. The adult butterfly emerges (4) after two to three weeks. The egg (5) is of the upright type. The caterpillar nibbles an opening at the top, through which it then climbs out.

43

Brimstone
Gonepteryx rhamni L.

The Brimstone inhabits the temperate regions of the Palaearctic from northern Africa through the whole of Europe and Asia to eastern Siberia. This striking butterfly, on the wing in early spring, is well known, but the greenish white female is often mistaken for a white and frequently escapes notice. Spring marks the end of the Brimstone's life span, which is very long — nearly a whole year. The butterfly emerges from the pupa in June or July and after a brief period of activity finds a hiding place where it passes a period of summer dormancy. After this it is on the wing again in early autumn, which often gives the impression of a second generation. In winter it hides in tree cavities, rock crevices, under stones and often also in leaves that have fallen to the ground. In spring it appears in woods when Lungwort, Noble Liverleaf and Primrose begin to flower. This is the most intensive period of its life. The butterflies copulate, and the females seek out food plants on which to lay the eggs. The green caterpillars that emerge from the eggs live for three to five weeks and then change into angular, green pupae. The life of the new generation begins two to three weeks later.

The Brimstone is not a very variable species, but 11 geographic forms have been described throughout its range differing in, for instance, shape of the wings, and size. With the encroachment of civilization it is rapidly declining in number. The exact reason for this is unknown but it seems likely that industrialization and the general pollution of the environment are responsible to a large extent.

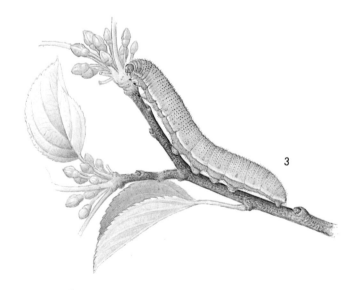

3

The Brimstone is one of the largest
sulphurs. Its wingspan measures
40—55 mm. The male (1) is lemon-yellow
without markings other than a reddish
spot in the centre of the wings. The
greenish white female (2) is more like
a white, particularly in flight. The
purplish antennae are typical. The
Brimstone has only one generation
a year. The butterflies are on the wing
from June until May of the following
year. Hence, it is an imago that
hibernates. The development of the
caterpillar (3) is very rapid and takes
place between May and June. It feeds on
Common Buckthorn and Alder
Buckthorn. The pupa (4) is held in
position by a girdle of strong fibre
encircling the twig and thorax and by the
cremaster, which is attached to the twig.

Purple Emperor
Apatura iris L.

Nymphalidae

These magnificent butterflies belong to the large family Nymphalidae, which comprises more than 4000 species found chiefly in the tropics. Europe, however, has some 70 relatively large species noted for their bright coloration. The Purple Emperor has special scales that refract light thus producing a metallic blue sheen that appears, to the observer, to pass from one wing to the other. This sheen is absent in females. The Purple Emperor is distributed from western Europe through the temperate regions of Asia to Japan. It inhabits spreading, broad-leaved forests. The butterflies are generally found alongside streams and rivers and by the edges of swampy places and ponds, where they often rest on the damp, muddy ground; they also settle on horse and cattle dung, or on the branches of shrubs overhanging the water. In the mountains they may be found even as high up as 1200 m.

The Lesser Purple Emperor (*Apatura ilia* D. et Sch.), is another spectacular European species. The wings of the males have a blue-violet sheen; in some forms the sheen is reddish violet. This species is found in places similar to those inhabited by the Purple Emperor but is more thermophilous. It is distributed in the Palaearctic region from Spain to Japan. A striking form is f. *clytie*, in which the wings of the males are coloured ochre with a reddish sheen.

Both the above species are becoming increasingly rare in the wild as a result of land reclamation, the regularisation of waterways and the spraying of riparian woods with pesticides to control mosquitoes.

The Purple Emperor has a wingspan of 55—65 cm. The male (1) differs from the female by the metallic sheen of his wings. There is one generation a year. The butterflies are on the wing from June till August. The caterpillars are active from August, hibernate over winter, and complete their development in spring. They feed on the leaves of various species of willow and on Aspen. The pupal stage (2) is very short — only two to three weeks beginning at the end of May.

The Lesser Purple Emperor (3) has a wingspan of 50—60 mm, in other words it is slightly smaller than the Purple Emperor. It, too, exhibits marked sexual dimorphism, similar to that of the preceding species. The butterflies are on the wing from June till August. The caterpillars (4) hibernate and feed on the same plants as do the caterpillars of the Purple Emperor. They have interesting, fork-shaped growths on the head (5). There is one generation a year.

1

5

3

4

47

Poplar Admiral
Limenitis populi L.

Nymphalidae

The Poplar Admiral is one of the largest and most attractive of European butterflies. The upper side of the wings is mostly velvety black with orange, blue and whitish spots. Only the female has prominent white spots on the forewings and a broad, white band on the hind wings. The underside of the wings, however, is a veritable kaleidoscope of bright colours the likes of which are not to be found elsewhere in Europe's fauna and which are reminiscent of the butterflies of the tropics. In the males of f. *tremulae* the white spots on the upperside of the wings are greatly reduced and may be practically invisible.

The Poplar Admiral occurs in woodland regions from France through all of Europe and Asia to Japan. It is found also in the more southerly parts of Scandinavia but is absent from the British Isles and southern Europe. It is an inhabitant of warm and damp flood plain woods where it may generally be found by pools. It may also be encountered in mountain valleys with lush vegetation alongside streams, up to altitudes of 1000—1100 m. On sunny mornings it settles on muddy forest rides. It is also fond of animal dung and other malodorous matter. Most of the day, however, it keeps to the sunny tree tops. Females in particular are seen only on the rare occasion. The Poplar Admiral was always a relatively rare butterfly and, unfortunately, in recent years has completely disappeared in some localities. It may be found only in places where its natural habitat has remained untouched or at least not drastically changed by man.

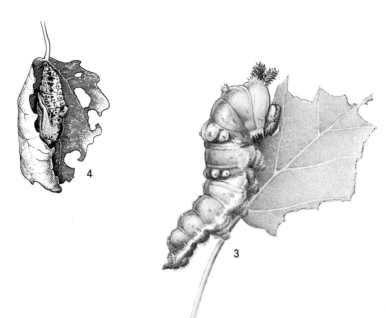

4

3

The Poplar Admiral has a wingspan of 65—80 mm. The females are on the average larger than the males (1, 2) and are also more strikingly coloured on the upperside of the wings. There is one generation a year. The butterflies are in flight in June and July. The caterpillars (3) feed on various species of poplar, chiefly Aspen, from summer until winter. Then they attach themselves to a leaf with a web of silken fibres and hibernate. The following spring in May, they complete their development and the adult butterflies emerge after a brief pupal stage (4).

White Admiral
Limenitis camilla L.

Nymphalidae

Though not exceptionally large the two illustrated species, with distinctive markings on the upper as well as underside of the wings, are both handsome butterflies. The White Admiral, coloured brownish black, has two rows of black spots on the outer underside margin of the hind wings. The very similar, darker Southern White Admiral (*L. reducta* Stgr.) has only one row of black spots and, in addition, bluish spots on the upperside of both pairs of wings.

The White Admiral's distribution from west to east is similar to that of the Poplar Admiral, i. e. from France to Japan. It is also found in southern England and on the southernmost edge of Sweden. In southern Europe it occurs also in Italy to 42° latitude north and locally in several places in the Mediterranean region (excepting the islands). In mountains it may be found at altitudes of up to 1500 m. The range of the Southern White Admiral is more southerly, embracing Spain and the whole Mediterranean region; in the east its limit is marked by the Caucasus and Iran and its northern boundary passes through the warmer regions of central Europe.

The butterflies of both species occur in open woods, chiefly in enclaves near brooks where they settle on the profuse thickets and flowering herbs. They are extremely wary and are quick fliers. The caterpillars feed on various species of honeysuckle and hibernate on shrubs. Their winter shelter, consisting of several dry leaves spun together, is called a hibernaculum. The caterpillar completes its development in spring and changes into a pupa of a rather unusual shape furnished with horns. Both species have been declining in number markedly in recent years, and in some localities the White Admiral as well as the Southern White Admiral have disappeared completely.

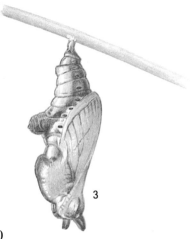

3

The White Admiral (1) has a wingspan of 45—52 mm. The coloration of the male and female is identical. There is one generation a year, and the butterflies are on the wing from May till July. The caterpillar (2) lives from summer until the following spring on honeysuckle and pupates suspended from a twig by the tip of the hind end. The butterfly emerges from the pupa (3) after two to three weeks.

The Southern White Admiral (4) has a wingspan of 45—50 mm. It is impossible to distinguish between the male and female by the coloration. There is one generation a year, although in the southern part of its range there may be two. Its development and food plants are the same as in the preceding species.

51

Hungarian Glider
Neptis rivularis Scop.

Nymphalidae

The genus *Neptis* F. has two thermophilous species in Europe. Both are distributed primarily in Asia, eastward to Japan. In the west the range of the Hungarian Glider extends in a narrow band to France. The range of the Common Glider (*Neptis sappho* Pall.), originally described from the southern Volga region, extends westwards only as far as eastern Austria and Czechoslovakia. The Hungarian Glider is on the wing in warm, thin, broad-leaved woods in lowland districts and hilly country up to altitudes of about 1000 m. The butterflies often congregate in damp places near brooks and springs, where they rest on the ground, on shrubs or on flowering plants. The butterfly is not particularly wary. It flies in gliding flight only on sunny days.

The Common Glider, which is similar but can be distinguished by the slightly different wing markings, inhabits warm, broad-leaved woods in lowland districts, chiefly oak woods with thick herbaceous undergrowth. In some places it occurs together with the Hungarian Glider.

Both species are true gems of nature and it is a pity that they are becoming increasingly rare due to the effects of civilization. The places where they do occur should be protected from insensitive management of the environment and from chemicals used in the control of forest pests. Otherwise the names of the Hungarian Glider and Common Glider will soon be entered in the Red Book of Endangered Species.

The Hungarian Glider (1) has a wingspan of 42—50 mm. The male and female have the same coloration. The coloration on the underside of the wings is striking (2).

There is one generation a year, with butterflies on the wing from late May until July, occasionally even until August. The caterpillar lives on *Spiraea* from late

3

52

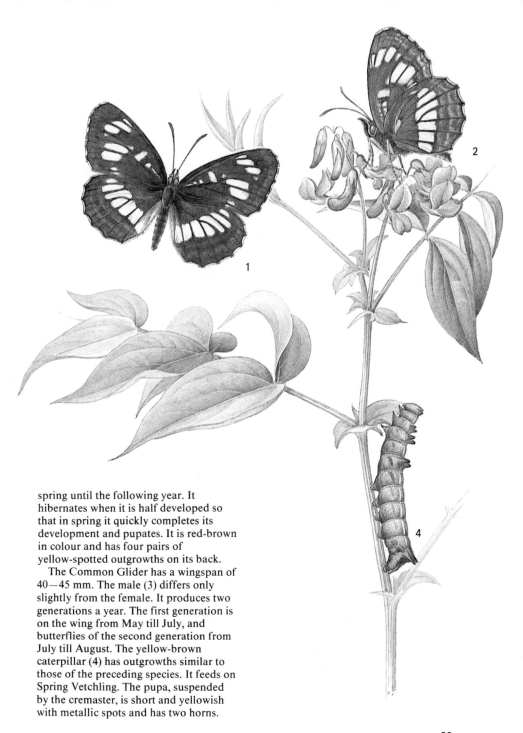

1

2

4

spring until the following year. It hibernates when it is half developed so that in spring it quickly completes its development and pupates. It is red-brown in colour and has four pairs of yellow-spotted outgrowths on its back.

The Common Glider has a wingspan of 40—45 mm. The male (3) differs only slightly from the female. It produces two generations a year. The first generation is on the wing from May till July, and butterflies of the second generation from July till August. The yellow-brown caterpillar (4) has outgrowths similar to those of the preceding species. It feeds on Spring Vetchling. The pupa, suspended by the cremaster, is short and yellowish with metallic spots and has two horns.

53

Peacock Butterfly
Inachis io L.

Nymphalidae

The Peacock is the best known of the 11 species of the subfamily Nymphalinae that are permanent inhabitants of Europe. It is one of the most popular of all butterflies because of its striking coloration and the conspicuous coloured 'eyes' on the wings resembling those on a peacock's tail feathers. This resemblance is reflected also in the common names by which it is known in various languages. Even its relative abundance has not diminished its popularity. One of the few species that has adapted to the changes in the landscape caused by civilization, it multiplies without trouble even in cities, on wasteland, dumps, in factory yards and similar places. Excluding the polar regions, it is distributed throughout all Europe and the temperate regions of Asia to Japan. In the north there is one generation a year, but in warmer regions there may be two. The butterflies, however, have a relatively long life span and may be encountered throughout the year. The imagos hibernate and may be found in winter in cellars, attics and other hiding places. In spring they are the first butterflies to be on the wing. Sunny weather often brings them out of their hiding places when there are still patches of snow on the ground. The butterflies regularly visit flowering Goat Willows, sun themselves on the trees and suck the nectar of the blossoms. The caterpillars are also striking, being black with white spots and branched spines over the whole body. They live communally on nettles, often stripping them completely of their leaves. The striking, pale green pupa hangs by its hind end on the stem or branch of a plant near the spot where the caterpillar spent the period of its development.

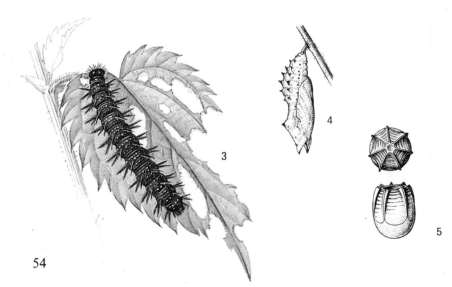

3

4

5

2

1

The Peacock Butterfly (1) has a wingspan of 50—60 mm. There is no difference in the coloration of the male and female. The wings are almost black on the underside (2). There are one or two generations a year. The butterflies are on the wing from March till June, and those of the new, second generation fly about from July till the following spring. Part of this time, mainly the winter months, is a quiescent period during which the butterfly rests in a concealed place. The caterpillars (3) feed communally on Stinging Nettle or Hop in May and June, sometimes also from July till September (those of the second generation). The pupal stage (4) is very brief, with the adult butterfly emerging after about one week. The eggs (5) are an unusual shape, viewed both from the side and from above.

55

Camberwell Beauty
Nymphalis antiopa L.

This handsome butterfly, one of the largest in Europe, inhabits woods and parks from lowland to mountain elevations, up to the forest line, which it reaches by way of damp mountain valleys. It has an extremely wide range: apart from the Mediterranean islands and southern Spain it is distributed throughout the broad-leaved woods of Europe, Asia and North America. The butterfly has a remarkably long life span. Except for late spring and early summer, when the caterpillars feed and the pupae rest, adult butterflies may be seen the whole year long. After several months of flying, some individuals are mere airborne wrecks with broken wings and faded colours. In spring, after hibernating, however, even in those that have survived more or less intact the border on the wings is much paler, more faded, than in summer when they emerged from the pupa. In the 1950s the Camberwell Beauty practically disappeared in central Europe but 20 years later its numbers began to increase again. The reason for this long-term fluctuation, however, remains unknown.

The Camberwell Beauty and the Large Tortoiseshell (*Nymphalis polychloros* L.) both hibernate as adult butterflies in caves, haylofts and the attics of rural dwellings. Both species are on the wing in spring, as soon as the weather becomes slightly warmer. They suck nectar from the blossoms of flowering Goat Willows or the sap oozing from wounded trees. In late summer, again, they regularly visit orchards to feed on the overripe fruit that has fallen to the ground. Both species are well suited to the experimental breeding of differently coloured forms: the colouring is caused by sudden changes in temperature occurring shortly before the butterfly emerges from the pupa.

The Camberwell Beauty (1) has a wingspan of 55—75 mm. There is one generation a year. The butterfly emerges in June and July, hibernates, and the female then lays her eggs in spring. The caterpillars (2) feed communally on willows, Sallow, birches and Aspen, completely stripping the branches of leaves. They disperse and wander away prior to pupation. The pupa (3) is of the

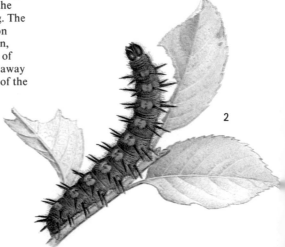

2

hanging type, and the butterfly emerges after two to three weeks.

The Large Tortoiseshell (4) has a wingspan of 50 to 55 mm. It, too, has but one generation a year, which has the same development as the Camberwell Beauty. The caterpillars (5) feed in spring on various trees and shrubs (willow, hazel, cherry, apricot), and are considered pests of fruit orchards because they also feed on fruit trees. However, like others, this butterfly has so declined in number that it will be necessary to protect rather than to destroy it.

Small Tortoiseshell
Aglais urticae L.

Nymphalidae

The Small Tortoiseshell is a common butterfly even in today's civilized world. So far it has successfully survived the erosion of its natural habitat, the smog of cities and industrial pollution. It is widespread from lowland to high mountain areas; it has been found as high as the 5000 m mark. A good flier, it ventures far afield in search of food. When the alpine meadows are in bloom it visits, in groups of up to 20 butterflies at a time, low flowering clumps of campions and pinks. The blossoms of hawkweed and ragwort are sometimes all occupied as well. The Small Tortoiseshell is distributed throughout Europe and Asia and visits even the polar tundra. The adult butterflies hibernate during the winter and may commonly be found in cellars, corridors and attics. A warm spell in winter sometimes brings them out from their shelter. On sunny spring days they often visit flowering Goat Willows.

Also widespread throughout the Palaearctic region of Europe and Asia (excepting the north) is the Comma Butterfly (*Polygonia c-album* L.). Its name is derived from the white pattern on the underside of the wings resembling the letter 'C' or a 'comma'. Here, too, the adult butterfly hibernates. A percentage of the population has only one generation, but some of the caterpillars develop rapidly into a second summer generation differing somewhat in coloration, and these are designated f. *hutchinsoni*. The colourful caterpillars and pupae are often found by hop pickers when they are harvesting the crop.

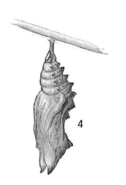

4

The Small Tortoiseshell (1) has a wingspan of 40—50 mm. There are two or three generations a year. These overlap so that there are adult butterflies on the wing almost continuously. The spiny, yellow-grey caterpillars (2) live communally on nettle in the wild as well as in city gardens, yards and waste places, in ditches, and at the edges of fields. When they are fully developed they hang by their abdomen (3) and pupate (4). There are no differences in coloration between the male and female nor between the generations during the course of the year. The Comma Butterfly (5, 6) has a wingspan of 42—50 mm.

There are one or two generations a year.
The imago hibernates. The caterpillars (7)
occur singly and feed on nettle, Hop,
Gooseberry and other plants. The male
and female are alike, but in general the
butterfly exhibits marked variability in
coloration and in the shape of the wings
(various deep lobes and scallops).

Red Admiral
Vanessa atalanta L.

Nymphalidae

The Red Admiral is one of the most handsome European butterflies. With its black wings and their bright red markings, it is comparable to the striking butterflies of the tropics. The dark underside of the wings with metallic glints is reminiscent of a rich brocade. In reality, however, this is excellent protective coloration. When the butterfly rests with closed wings on the trunk of a tree, it is practically invisible. And when it suddenly spreads its wings, revealing the fiery red markings, the enemy halts momentarily in surprise and the butterfly makes its escape. The Red Admiral is native to northern Africa and southern Europe, its range extending eastwards to central Asia. In summer it temporarily inhabits the whole of Europe. In central Europe it is not a permanent resident but flies there every year from the south and sometimes multiplies in such numbers that in late summer it is very abundant. However, it rarely hibernates with success north of the Alps.

The related Painted Lady (*Vanessa cardui* L.) is also a well-known migrant. It is distributed throughout the world except for South America. However, it is native to the tropical and subtropical regions, where it may cause damage to agricultural crops, e. g. on orange plantations. From here it journeys every year to all parts of Europe, even to Great Britain and Scandinavia. It has also been seen in Iceland and occasionally captures the attention of ship passengers on the open sea.

The Red Admiral (1, 2) has a wingspan of 50—60 mm. The male and female have like coloration, the same as in the following species. The butterflies are on the wing from May until autumn for individuals from the various waves of

5

3

immigration intermingle with the local offspring. The caterpillars, which take about a month to develop, also may be found throughout the growing season. They feed on Stinging Nettle, are sluggish, and lead a solitary life concealed in furled nettle leaves.

The Painted Lady (3) has a wingspan
of 45—60 mm. The butterflies arrive from
the south between April and June and
their offspring are on the wing until
October. The caterpillars (4) may be
encountered from June till September.
They feed on thistle, burdock, Stinging
Nettle and other wild as well as
cultivated plants. The grey-green pupae
(5) resemble those of other species of
vanessids.

Map Butterfly
Araschnia levana L.

Nymphalidae

This smallest of European vanessids is noteworthy for the beautiful coloration of the underside of the wings. The male and female are alike, but the various generations differ in coloration. The first generation, f. *levana* L., which is on the wing in spring, has bright reddish brown wings with black markings; the summer generation, f. *prorsa* L., has black wings with yellow-white bands and very variable spots. In warm years there may also be a third generation, f. *porima* O., with a coloration that is intermediate to those of the two other forms. The pupa hibernates.

In experiments with artificially induced conditions it was discovered that the colouring of the butterflies depends on the amount of daylight during the period of the caterpillar's development. When it develops in late spring and early summer when the days are long, the resulting form is f. *prorsa*. If the development takes place in autumn when there are fewer hours of daylight, then the butterflies that emerge are the form *levana*.

The Map Butterfly is widespread in the temperate regions from France through Europe and Asia to Japan. It is absent from warm, southern regions such as Spain, Italy and Greece, and from the British Isles and Scandinavia. It is found in open woods and meadows along the banks of brooks and rivers. In mountains it occurs only up to heights of approximately 1000 m. Although the food plant of the caterpillar is the ubiquitous Stinging Nettle, it is interesting to note that this species, unlike the Small Tortoiseshell, which also feeds on nettles, has not succeeded in adapting to life in the city.

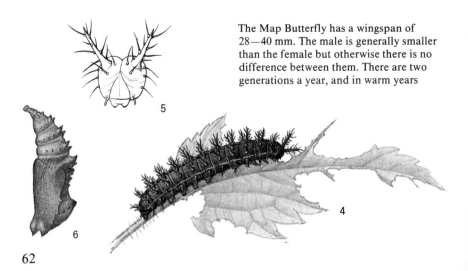

The Map Butterfly has a wingspan of 28—40 mm. The male is generally smaller than the female but otherwise there is no difference between them. There are two generations a year, and in warm years

5

6

4

also a partial third generation. The first
generation (f. *levana*, fig. 1) butterflies are
on the wing in April and May; the second
generation (f. *prorsa*, figs. 2 and 3) from
July to September; and the third
generation from September to October.
The caterpillars (4) live gregariously on
the Stinging Nettle; their development
takes about four weeks, and they have
a typically spiny head (5). The pupa (6) is
brown and its hind end is curved
sidewards.

63

Queen of Spain Fritillary
Issoria lathonia L.

Of the less than 30 European species of the subfamily Brenthinae the Queen of Spain Fritillary is the only migrant. A superb flier, it appears every year even in regions where it is not a permanent resident, e. g. in the British Isles and in Scandinavia beyond the Arctic Circle. Otherwise its range includes northern Africa, all of Europe and Asia to the Himalayas and China. It is a steppe to forest-steppe species that is partial to arid slopes, field paths, expanses of bare earth and sandbanks. It is fond of resting and sunning itself on sunbaked earth. The flowers it visits most are thistles (*Carduus* and *Cirsium*), the Cornflower and scabiouses (*Knautia* and *Scabiosa*).

The two sexes have the same colouring, but the female is much larger than the male. There is also a slight difference between the spring and summer generations both in size and coloration. Butterflies of the spring generation are smaller and have a large greenish expanse at the base of the wing. Butterflies of the summer generation are larger and more reddish. The lustrous pearly spots on the underside of the hind wings (2) have a brighter sheen than those of any other fritillaries. Sometimes the spots even merge to form continuous bands (f. *paradoxa*). The Queen of Spain Fritillary hibernates in central Europe only in small numbers. The population is augmented every year by arrivals from the south. The butterflies of the second, summer generation are often quite numerous as well.

4

The Queen of Spain Fritillary (1, 2) has a wingspan of 35—45 mm. In the northern parts of its range there are one or two generations, either augmented by or consisting solely of arrivals from the south. In southern Europe there are two or three generations. The butterflies are on the wing from April till June and again from July till September. The first

generation caterpillars (3) develop from
May till July, those of the second
generation from August, after which they
hibernate and then complete their
development in spring. The food plants
are various species of violet; also listed
are *Onobrychis* and *Anchusa*. The pupa (4)
hangs upside down on or close by the
food plant.

65

Silver-washed Fritillary
Argynnis paphia L.

The genus *Argynnis* was established by the Danish zoologist J. C. Fabricius in 1807. It was later divided by various scientists into several separate genera, for example *Pandoriana, Argyronome, Fabriciana* and *Mesoacidalia*. Of the European fritillaries only the Silver-washed remained in the original genus. This is a large, striking butterfly, which flies about in the middle of summer in forest margins, woodland clearings, glades and alongside brooks. It is most abundant in lowland districts but makes its way via valleys to relatively high altitudes in the mountains — up to approximately 1700 m. Flowering thistles and Hemp Agrimony with these butterflies perched on the blooms are a typical feature of European summers. What with the inroads of civilization and more intensive forestry, however, this species is gradually disappearing. Areas where it remains abundant have diminished greatly in number. An interesting aspect of its general distribution is that there is a small, isolated group in Algeria (north Africa). Otherwise, excepting southern Spain, the northern parts of the British Isles and Scandinavia, it is distributed throughout the whole of Europe and the temperate regions of Asia to Japan.

The male (1) differs from the female (2) by having bands of scent scales along the veins on the forewings. In addition, the female is usually larger and darker. Often much darker individuals — the form *valesina* — are encountered among the normally coloured females. The silver colouring on the underside (3) is in bands on the greenish expanse of the wing.

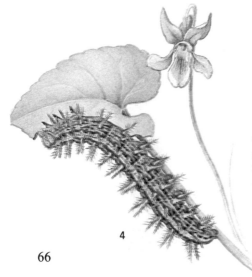

4

The Silver-washed Fritillary (1, 2, 3) has a wingspan of 55—65 mm. It exhibits marked sexual dimorphism. There is one generation a year. The adult butterflies are on the wing from June till September, although they are most abundant in late July and early August. The caterpillar (4) lives from August, hibernates, and then

changes into a pupa (5) in May. It feeds
on the leaves of various species of violets
and is active at night. It is coloured black
with yellow longitudinal stripes and has
the branched spines typical of the
caterpillars of the Nymphalid family.
This handsome butterfly will apparently
soon require protection.

Dark Green Fritillary
Mesoacidalia aglaja L.

Nymphalidae

Of this trio of similar species, which are now classified in two different genera, the Dark Green Fritillary is the most common and most widely known. It is distributed throughout all of Europe and in Asia as far as Japan. In Africa it occurs in one place in Morocco. It is generally found in the forest zone, mostly in lowland and hilly districts, but occurs also high up in the mountains to 2000 m. Its favourite haunts are grassy forest clearings, forest rides, meadows and grassy banks, where it wings its way in fluttering flight, alighting every now and then on the low flowering vegetation, on both leaves and flowers. It is found most often on the flowers of the Bramble, Cornflower, Wild Thyme etc. Characteristic features of this butterfly are the round silvery spots on the underside of the greenish hind wings (2). The female is larger than the male and the underside of her wings is darker.

The High Brown Fritillary (*Fabriciana adippe* D. et. Sch.) and the Niobe Fritillary (*Fabriciana niobe* L.) have more or less the same range as the Dark Green Fritillary but are not found in northern Europe; the Niobe Fritillary is absent also from northern Africa. In the mountains, however, they occur at elevations up to 3000 m. They are less common species, particularly the Niobe Fritillary. The best means of identifying these fritillaries is by the underside of the wings, where one can see at a glance the differences in the arrangement of the silvery spots and in the pattern of the other markings. The High Brown Fritillary often occurs as the form *cleodoxa*, in which the silvery spots on the underside of the hind wing are absent.

The Niobe Fritillary (5) has a wingspan of 42—55 mm. It tends to occur in the dark form, particularly in the mountains. The occurrence of the caterpillar and the plants it feeds on are the same as for the Dark Green Fritillary and High Brown Fritillary.

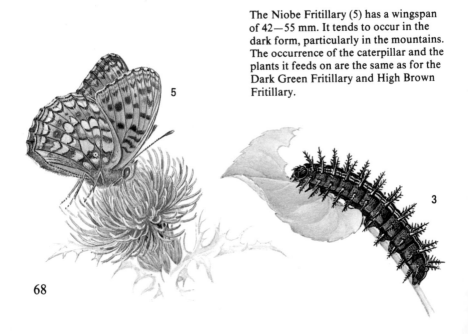

5

3

The Dark Green Fritillary (1,2) has
a wingspan of 50—55mm and is marked
by sexual dimorphism. There is one
generation a year, with the butterflies on
the wing from June till August. The
caterpillar (3) develops from August and
hibernates. It completes its development
in May of the following year and then
pupates. It is black, spiny and has red
spots on the sides of its body. It feeds on
various species of violet and is active at
night. The pupal stage lasts about
a month.

The High Brown Fritillary (4) has
a wingspan of 42—55 mm. The difference
between the male and female is less
striking than in the Dark Green Fritillary.
It is a very variable species, both
individually and zoogeographically.
Several geographic forms have been
described, e. g. ssp. *chlorodippe* H. S., ssp.
auresiana Fruh., ssp. *norvegica* Schulz.

69

Lesser Marbled Fritillary
Brenthis ino Rott.

Nymphalidae

Of the smaller fritillaries some 20 species are native to Europe. At first glance they all appear to be very similar, but their morphological features, primarily the anatomy of the external copulatory organs, fit several separate genera. The various species are best distinguished by the coloration and markings on the underside of the hind wings. The Lesser Marbled Fritillary has a scattered distribution throughout all Europe and lives in Asia as far as Japan; it is not found in the warm Mediterranean region, the British Isles or the northernmost parts of Scandinavia. It inhabits damp meadows and the edges of moors, which are generally found at high altitudes and in cooler regions. In many places, however, the drainage of wet meadows, and hence the disappearance of its natural habitat, has caused a marked decline in its numbers. Where once this butterfly was fairly common it is becoming quite rare and deserves to be protected by law.

The Cranberry Fritillary (*Boloria aquilonaris* Stich.) occurs only sporadically in central Europe, on moors. Its distribution becomes continuous in the tundra regions of northern Europe. In Asia its distribution has not been sufficiently investigated as yet. The existence of this butterfly in central Europe is dependent on the moors being preserved in their natural state. The Bog Fritillary (*Proclossiana eunomia* Esp.) likewise has a sporadic distribution in central Europe, where it exists as a relict of the glacial period. Elsewhere it occurs in northern Europe, northern Asia and North America.

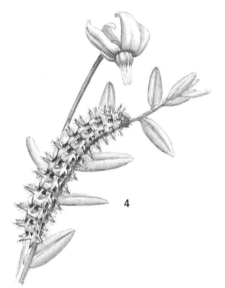

4

The Lesser Marbled Fritillary (1, 2) has a wingspan of 32—40 mm. There is no difference in coloration between the male and female nor sexual dimorphism. There is one generation a year, with the butterflies on the wing in June and July. The caterpillar is found from September until the following May on burnet, Wood Goat's-beard, and various brambles. Sometimes the egg hibernates and the caterpillar does not develop until spring.

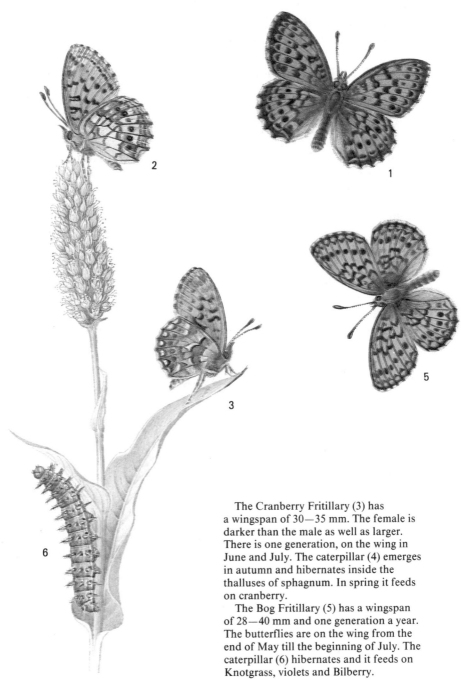

The Cranberry Fritillary (3) has
a wingspan of 30—35 mm. The female is
darker than the male as well as larger.
There is one generation, on the wing in
June and July. The caterpillar (4) emerges
in autumn and hibernates inside the
thalluses of sphagnum. In spring it feeds
on cranberry.

The Bog Fritillary (5) has a wingspan
of 28—40 mm and one generation a year.
The butterflies are on the wing from the
end of May till the beginning of July. The
caterpillar (6) hibernates and it feeds on
Knotgrass, violets and Bilberry.

Small Pearl-bordered Fritillary
Clossiana selene D. et Sch.

Nymphalidae

This small fritillary was first described in the environs of Vienna. In the early nineteenth century there were several scientists residing in that city who figured prominently in the history of butterfly research. They described species found in the immediate vicinity of Vienna. Many of these localities, however, were engulfed long ago by the expanding city.

The Small Pearl-bordered Fritillary is distributed throughout all Europe, except the warm Mediterranean region, and in Asia, and is also reported from North America. It is found in meadows and in grassy woodland margins and clearings from lowland districts to the alpine belt to altitudes of about 2400 m. It is very variable in coloration and there is a tendency for the species to produce very dark forms with reduced brown-red colouring.

The very similar Pearl-bordered Fritillary (*Clossiana euphrosyne* L.) differs from the preceding species primarily by the shape and arrangement of the spots on the underside of the hind wings. It has a similar range but is not reported from North America and in Europe extends farther south.

The Violet Fritillary (*Clossiana dia* L.) has the hind wings beautifully coloured on the underside, and this is what distinguishes it best from other similar species. The black markings on the upperside are also much more prominent than in other species. It is a butterfly of the forest-steppe and is distributed throughout the temperate regions of Europe and Asia to western China.

The Small Pearl-bordered Fritillary (1, 2) has a wingspan of 28—38 mm. There is no difference in coloration between the male and female. There are one or two generations a year, depending on the altitude and climate. The butterfly is on the wing from May till July. The caterpillars hibernate and may be encountered throughout the year, for the generations overlap. They feed on violets, Wild Strawberry and other plants. The pupal stage lasts three to four weeks.

The Pearl-bordered Fritillary (3) has a wingspan of 32—40 mm. There are one or two generations a year, which are on the wing from April till July (depending on the altitude) and from August till

4

September. The caterpillar hibernates and pupates the following spring.

The Violet Fritillary (4) has a wingspan of 27—35 mm. The female is slightly larger than the male but there is no difference in coloration. There are two or

three generations a year, which overlap, and thus adult butterflies may be found from April till October. The caterpillar feeds on plants similar to those of the foregoing species.

Spotted Fritillary
Melitaea didyma Esp.

It is not easy to identify the 15 European species of the genera *Melitaea* F. and *Mellicta* Billb. In many instances the markings on the underside of the wings will prove a handy aid, but in other instances the only sure means of identification is by examining the copulatory organs, which are rather complex in butterflies of these genera. The Spotted Fritillary was formerly abundant in warm, dry, grassy localities in forest-steppes. Over the last decades, however, it has vanished from many of its habitats and has become relatively rare. It is distributed in northern Africa, southern and central Europe and in the east to central Asia. The butterfly is strikingly coloured. Males are a bright, brownish red with black spots, females are extremely variable. Some resemble the males; often their number includes individuals with some yellowish spots or with more extensive dark markings. In some the brownish red colour completely disappears beneath the grey and black tone. The colouring varies also according to locality and hence several geographical forms have been described.

The Glanville Fritillary (*Melitaea cinxia* L.) has a similar range but extends farther north and eastwards as far as the Amur River. It was described according to the Swedish populations. It is more damp-loving, fond of shrubby meadows and not as abundant as the Spotted Fritillary, even in suitable biotopes. Furthermore its coloration is not as variable. It is readily identified by the markings on the underside of the hind wings.

4

The Spotted Fritillary (1) has a wingspan of 30—40 mm. There are marked differences between the sexes. The colouring on the underside of the wings is characteristic (2). There are one or two generations a year, depending on the climate. The butterflies are on the wing from May till June and again from July till August. The caterpillar (3) develops very rapidly in June; second generation caterpillars hibernate. Their food plants include speedwell, plantain, Wormwood, toadflax and Yellow Woundwort *(Stachys recta)*. The pupal stage (4) lasts about two weeks.

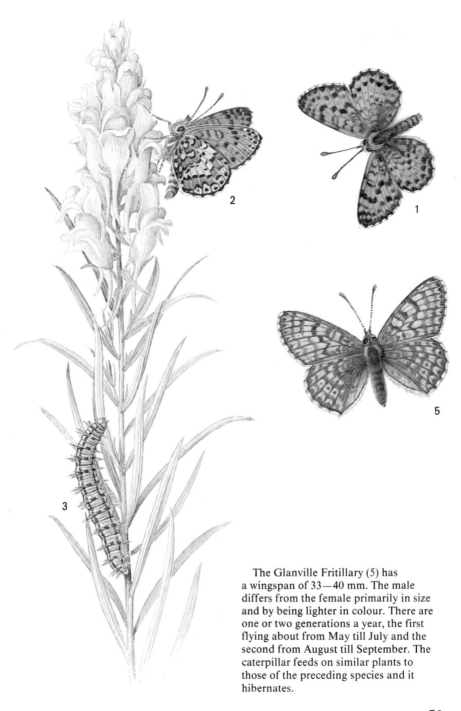

The Glanville Fritillary (5) has
a wingspan of 33—40 mm. The male
differs from the female primarily in size
and by being lighter in colour. There are
one or two generations a year, the first
flying about from May till July and the
second from August till September. The
caterpillar feeds on similar plants to
those of the preceding species and it
hibernates.

Heath Fritillary
Mellicta athalia Rott.

The Heath Fritillary is the most widespread and abundant species of the *Melitaea* and *Mellicta*. It inhabits the entire Palaearctic region from western Europe to Japan, being absent only from northern Africa. In the British Isles it is found in several areas in the south of England. In mountains it may be encountered up to altitudes of 2000 m. The butterflies may be seen in flowering meadows, forest-steppe, forest margins and similar places. This is a very variable species, both individually and geographically, and is therefore difficult to distinguish from similar species (e. g. *M. britomartis* Assm., *M. aurelia* Nick. and *M. diamina* Lang.). In steppes the butterflies are often very small; in damp habitats and moors they are brightly and darkly coloured. Often they can be distinguished only by microscopic examination of anatomical features. Many species native to Europe and several native to Asia have been described within the overall range; there is even the possibility that the species contains a sister species differing in the ecology of the larval stages. All this will perhaps be investigated some day, assuming, of course, that the Heath Fritillary survives the present encroachment of civilization. Where formerly tens and even hundreds of these butterflies could commonly be seen assembled on puddles in fields or on the moist soil beside brooks sucking up water, nowadays this is a very rare sight. The Heath Fritillary is disappearing, probably because of environmental pollution, even from localities such as protected landscape areas and national parks.

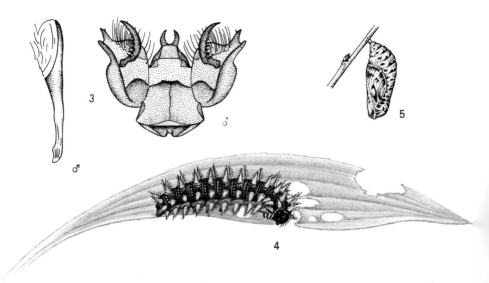

3

♂

♂

5

4

The Heath Fritillary (1) has a wingspan of 25—38 mm. There is no difference in coloration between the male and female. Typical features are the pattern on the underside of the wings (2), and also the copulatory organs (3). There are two generations a year, although these are sometimes considered to be a single extended generation. The butterflies may be encountered in the wild continuously from May until September. Likewise caterpillars (4) of varying ages may be found simultaneously and this makes it impossible to distinguish between generations, if there should be more than one. The larval stage is the stage of hibernation. The caterpillar feeds on plantain, cow-weed, Cornflower and other meadowland herbs. The butterfly emerges from the pupa (5) after one to two weeks.

77

Scarce Fritillary
Euphydryas maturna L.

Nymphalidae

Europe is the home of six species of the genus *Euphydryas* Scudd. but only two, the Scarce Fritillary (*E. maturna* L.) and the Marsh Fritillary (*E. aurinia* Rott.), are comparatively widely distributed. The others have a scattered distribution in high mountains districts — either in northern Europe or in the west Mediterranean region, on both the African and European continents. The Scarce Fritillary is found in Europe north of the Alps, but its distribution is discontinuous because it inhabits damp lowland and riparian forests that are not found in mountainous or dry regions. This handsome, strikingly coloured butterfly is a veritable gem, but conditions for its existence are continually deteriorating. Nowadays it occurs in greater numbers only in isolated localities and despite strict protection is in danger of becoming extinct in some countries.

The caterpillar takes two years to complete its development. It hibernates twice, which is very unusual for butterflies. The female lays the eggs in a cluster and the caterpillars remain together in the communal nest at first; they also hibernate there the first time. Only after hibernation do they separate, hibernating the second time singly when nearly fully grown. In the spring of the third year they feed for a brief period and then pupate. The pupa hangs by the cremaster head down, and the butterfly emerges two weeks later. The butterflies are on the wing only on sunny days. They alight on the white flowers of umbelliferous plants and privet and on the foliage of trees and shrubs. They have a relatively short life span of 10—14 days, just long enough to fulfill their purpose of producing another generation.

4

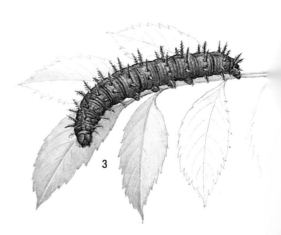

3

The Scarce Fritillary has a wingspan of
35—42 mm. The male (1) is smaller than
the female (2) and more brightly
coloured. One generation takes two years

1

2

to develop, which means that the
butterflies encountered each year belong
to alternating generations. They are on
the wing in May and June. The
development of the caterpillar (3) lasts
until the spring of the third year. At first
it feeds on the Aspen and other poplars,
later on plantain, Field Scabious,
speedwell, ash seedlings and other plants.
It is black and spiny, sometimes with
yellow spots on the back and sides. The
pupa (4) is black and white.

Marbled White
Melanargia galathea L.

Satyridae

Of the six species of *Melanargia* Meig. found in Europe only the Marbled White is fairly widely distributed. Excluding the northern regions it inhabits all of Europe, including southern England, northern Africa, and in the east its range extends as far as the Caucasus. Related species are found in quite small areas in southern Europe and northern Africa, also locally here and there in Asia.

The Marbled White was described according to a specimen from central Europe. However, it is a very variable species and there are many relatively different geographic forms throughout its range, e. g. ssp. *lachesis* Hb. in southern France and ssp. *lucasi* Rmbr. in northern Africa. The individuals also vary a lot. Some specimens are richly patterned in brown to black on a yellowish white ground, occasionally dusted a darker colour (f. *procida*), and a form with yellow ground colouring is not unusual either.

The Marbled White is found in rather dry meadows, forest-steppes, forest margins and grassy clearings and also in waste places near housing developments and by the roadside, that is if it has not been exterminated by pesticides. This is also the main reason why it is disappearing from farmlands. However, what also contributes to the general decline in its numbers is global pollution from industrial emissions and waste. Although this butterfly may be encountered at altitudes of up to 2000 m (in southern Europe) or 1500 m (in central Europe), the centre of its distribution is in lowland and hilly districts, particularly in regions with diverse vegetation and interrupted forests.

4

The antennae are only slightly thickened at the tip and the labial palps are S-shaped (3). There is one generation a year, which flies about for a relatively long time, from June till August. The females are on the wing somewhat later than the males. The caterpillar's development is slow in summer and full growth is attained only after hibernation. It feeds on various grasses such as cat's-tail, brome, Soft Grass, Common Couch and meadow-grass. It pupates in May and June. The pupa (4) has two black spots at the front. It lies loose on the ground, usually in a clump of grass. The butterfly emerges after about a month.

The Marbled White (1) has a wingspan of 37—52 mm. The female is larger than the male, and the markings on the underside of her wings are not as prominent (2).

80

1

2

3

81

Great Banded Grayling
Brintesia circe F.

Satyridae

The family of browns has some 1500 known species worldwide; of these approximately 100 are found in Europe. Opinions as to the position of this family differ widely. Some authorities class it as a mere subfamily — the Satyrinae — of the family Nymphalidae. Its members are moderately large to quite large butterflies tied almost exclusively to grasses. They often inhabit very rugged areas at the very limits of life's existence, such as high mountain biotopes near permanent snow and ice, polar regions or, at the other extreme, arid rocks, sandbanks and the edges of deserts.

The Great Banded Grayling is the largest European brown. Its range includes the warm parts of Europe and Asia and extends to the Himalayas. Absent at higher mountain levels, it is found in forest-steppes, particularly in dry oak woods, where it likes to rest on branches or on the thick oak trunks. The colouring of the underside of the wings closely resembles this background (2) (an example of protective coloration) so that when the wings are closed the butterfly is practically invisible. Of interest in large species of browns is their territorial instinct, with the males defending their territory against others of the same species.

Similar warm habitats are also frequented by the less striking Woodland Grayling (*Hipparchia fagi* Sc.), whose distribution in Europe and way of life are practically the same as those of the Great Banded Grayling.

The Great Banded Grayling has a wingspan of 55—65 mm. The female is larger than the male (1, 2) and has more prominent pale bands on the wings. There is one generation a year, which is on the wing in June and July. The butterflies have a gliding flight and are so wary that one must not even try to get near them. When the sun is not shining they rest in concealed places. The spindle-shaped, prominently striped caterpillar develops from summer until it hibernates and then continues its development the following year until June. It feeds on grasses, chiefly Rye-grass and brome, and is active at night. The pupa is plump and coloured

2

reddish brown with yellow spots. It rests loose on the ground. The butterfly emerges after two to three weeks.

The Woodland Grayling has a wingspan of 60—70 mm. The female is more vividly coloured and is larger than the male (3). The first pair of legs is atrophied (4) and much smaller than the other pairs (5). There is one generation a year. The butterflies are on the wing from June till August. The caterpillar begins its development in summer and completes it the following June. It feeds on Soft Grass, fescue and other grasses.

Grayling
Hipparchia semele L.

Except for several islands in the Mediterranean and northern Scandinavia this species is distributed throughout the whole of Europe, its range extending approximately as far as Armyanskaya (Armenia). Its further distribution in eastern Asia has not been investigated as yet. The Grayling is a butterfly of lower altitudes and is found in the mountains only occasionally. Although it was formerly a relatively common butterfly of field and steppes, it is now an endangered species and occurs only locally. It demonstrates a preference for sandy and loamy banks, where it settles on the ground and basks in the sun. When the wings are closed (2) it blends perfectly with its background and is difficult to find, even if one has watched where it landed. Several geographical forms have been described within its range of distribution and even populations in various areas may differ slightly according to the local climate.

In very warm habitats, chiefly on stony banks, rocks and in rocky steppes, one may also encounter the Hermit (*Chazara briseis* L.) along with the Grayling. The Hermit is distributed in northern Africa, central and southern Europe and in Asia to the Altai Mountains and the Pamir. It is one of the most variable butterflies and within its range there are many geographic forms differing not only in size but also in the extent of the pale markings on the dark wings. Of the individual forms f. *pirata* is noteworthy: the females have orange instead of pale markings.

The Grayling (1, 2) has a wingspan of 48—55 mm. It exhibits marked sexual dimorphism. The male is brownish without prominent markings on the underside of the wings. The females (1) have ochre-yellow markings on the wings and are thus much more colourful. There is one generation a year, but the butterflies are on the wing a long time, from July till September. The caterpillar (3) hibernates and is fully grown in June. It feeds on various grasses, mostly hair-grass, Sheep's Fescue and meadow-grass.

5

The Hermit (4, 5) has a wingspan of 45—60 mm. The female (4) is larger and more vividly coloured than the male. There is one generation a year. The butterflies are on the wing from June till September but are most abundant in late summer. The development of the caterpillar is the same as in the preceding species. It feeds on various species of *Sesleria* and other thermophilous grasses.

85

Dryad
Minois dryas Sc.

Satyridae

This interesting butterfly is distributed in the temperate regions of Europe and across the whole of Asia to Japan. The European range is bounded by approximately the 42nd and 54th parallels of latitude north, so that the Dryad occurs only in the northern part of the Iberian Peninsula, but is not found in central and southern Spain. It is absent also from the British Isles and Scandinavia; only in the Baltic states does it extend somewhat farther north. In the Mediterranean region it is absent from the islands, a large part of Italy and from Greece. In Europe it thus has a scattered distribution; in its relatively circumscribed localities, however, it may occasionally be quite plentiful. It may be found on shrubby hillsides, in grassy woodland clearings, in forest-steppes and in heaths from lowland districts to altitudes of about 1500 m.

The Dryad's flight is very typical with the butterfly bounding up and down in the air. When it is flying it appears to be a striking black butterfly, but in reality it is dark brown with blue eyespots rimmed with black on the forewings. It often rests on clumps of flowering Wild Thyme, the blossoms of Marjoram and other plants that flower in the height of summer. In many localities where it was formerly abundant this lovely butterfly is, alas, now extinct, and in the places where it remains its chances of surviving are negligible.

The Dryad has a wingspan of 45—60 mm. The female (1) is larger than the male (2) and has more distinct eyespots on the wings. The butterflies (as in other species of browns) have the veins enlarged at the base of the wings to form inflated vesicles (3). The butterflies of the single generation are on the wing from July till September. The caterpillar (4)

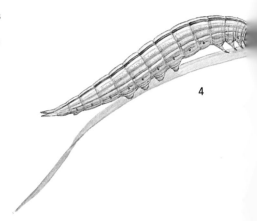

4

hibernates and then pupates between May and June. It is yellowish grey with brown stripes on the sides and is active at night. It feeds on various grasses, mostly tall oat-grass. The pupa is brown with a paler hind end. It rests on the ground in a loose cocoon.

2

1

3

Scotch Argus or Northern Brown
Erebia aethiops Esp.

Satyridae

The more than 40 European species of the genus *Erebia* form a distinct group of butterflies in general and within the family of Satyrids as well. The individual species are very similar in appearance. They are relatively small to moderately large butterflies coloured blackish brown with more or less prominent eyespots by the outer edge on the upperside as well as the underside of the wings. Their ecological requirements are also unusual. Most live in high mountains. Some species are natives of polar regions with as harsh conditions as in the mountains. Only a few inhabit warmer regions and may be found even in lowland districts. One such is the Scotch Argus. In Europe it occurs nowhere in the north except in Scotland, and it is likewise absent from the Mediterranean region. Otherwise it is distributed throughout the temperate zone from France to Siberia. It generally occurs in hilly country, in open woods and on slopes up to as high as 2000 m.

Another species of mid-altitudes is the Arran Brown (*Erebia ligea* L.), which is restricted to wooded valleys with lush vegetation up to altitudes of about 1000 m. It is distributed from France to Japan and is found also in Scandinavia. However, it is absent from the flat country in the northern parts of Germany. Found at higher levels, in the spruce belt, is the very similar Large Ringlet (*Erebia euryale* Esp.), which is more brightly coloured on the underside of the wings. It has a scattered distribution in the European mountains but is absent from northern Europe. Eastwards its range extends as far as the Altai Mountains.

The Scotch Argus (1) has a wingspan of 37—48 mm. The male and female are very similar. The coloration of the upperside and underside of the wing is the same. Butterflies of the one generation are in flight from July till the beginning of August, depending on the altitude. The caterpillar hibernates. Its food plants are Annual Meadow-grass, Cocksfoot, Velvet Bent etc.

4

88

The Arran Brown (2, 3) has a wingspan
of 37—45 mm and usually white
markings on the underside of the hind
wings (3). The female is larger than the
male and has more prominent eyespots
on the wings. The single generation is on
the wing from June till August. The
caterpillar feeds on Crab-grass and millet
and hibernates.

1

3

2

The Large Ringlet (4) has a wingspan
of 33—40 mm. It resembles the preceding
species, but is more vividly coloured on
the underside of the wings, particularly
the female. The butterflies of the one
generation are on the wing in July and
August. The caterpillar feeds on various
mountain grasses.

Mountain Ringlet
Erebia epiphron Knoch.

Satyridae

The Mountain Ringlet is a typical representative of the mountain fauna of Europe. It is found nowhere else. It is absent from Finland and Scandinavia, occurs in a limited area in Scotland and in the hills of England, and is otherwise distributed in the Pyrenees, Alps, Carpathians and Balkan mountains at altitudes of 1000—2000 m. Its scattered, isolated distribution has led to the evolution of several geographical forms differing in size and markings. The Mountain Ringlet is one of many species of the genus *Erebia* that inhabit the mountains of Europe. Some of these are found only in the Alps, in isolated localities. They are adapted to the harsh mountain conditions and are able to adjust even to a sudden drop in temperature and snowstorms in the middle of summer. The caterpillars are likewise adapted to the rigours of this environment and feed on the tough mountain grasses. Often they do not complete their development in a single season and then this continues the following year after hibernation.

The other two illustrated species are also mountain butterflies found at even higher altitudes. The Dewy Ringlet (*Erebia pandrose* Bkh.) occurs at between 1600 and 3000 m. Only in Norway, beyond the Arctic Circle, does it descend to the sea. It is found also in the mountains of central Asia. A very variable species it forms strikingly coloured subspecies in the various mountain ranges. The Silky Ringlet (*Erebia gorge* Hb.), like the preceding ringlet, occurs at heights of 1500—3000 m in the mountains of Europe. It is partial to rocky places and screes and settles on the mountain flowers growing in the grass between the rocks and stones.

The Mountain Ringlet (1) has a wingspan of 30—35 mm. There is not much difference between the male and female, although in the female the zone with eyespots on the upperside of the wings is more prominent. There is one generation a year, which flies in July and August. The caterpillar begins its development in the autumn and completes it the following spring. It feeds on various grasses, chiefly Tufted Hair-grass.

The Dewy Ringlet (2) has a wingspan of 38—45 mm. The female is larger than the male and has more eyespots on the wings. In addition the underside of her wings has more contrasting colouring (3).

There is one generation a year. The
butterflies fly on sunny days in July and
August. The caterpillar feeds on grasses.

The Silky Ringlet (4) has a wingspan of
35—40 mm. Typical of this butterfly is
the coloration of the underside of the
wings (5). Its flying period and the
development of the caterpillar are the
same as in the foregoing species.

91

Meadow Brown
Maniola jurtina L.

Satyridae

To this day the Meadow Brown continues to be one of the commonest of European butterflies. It may be seen flying in meadows, forest margins, grassy woodland clearings and forest-steppe. It is also one of the few inhabitants of pasturelands and various grassy waste places such as city parks, playgrounds, roadside ditches, railway embankments and weirs. The flight of this medium sized, inconspicuously coloured butterfly is relatively slow and fluttering, and it frequently alights on the various meadow flowers. The markings on the wings are very variable and some individuals even tend towards albinism; these are generally only partial albinos. The Meadow Brown is distributed throughout practically all of Europe and in northern Africa. It is absent only from northern Scandinavia. The Ural region is considered to be the eastern limit of its range.

The related Dusky Meadow Brown (*Hyponephele lycaon* Kühn) is distributed from Spain through central and southern Europe to central Asia. It is more thermophilous and less common than the Meadow Brown. It is partial to dry, grassy biotopes. Apparently it is not as adaptable and hence has disappeared from many places in the past decades. The Gatekeeper (*Pyronia tithonus* L.) also is gradually becoming a rare species in Europe. Its range extends from Spain to the Caucasus and includes the British Isles, but it is not found in northeastern Europe.

The Meadow Brown has a wingspan of 40—48 mm. It exhibits marked sexual dimorphism. The male (1) is brown, the female (2) more brightly coloured. There is one generation a year and very occasionally two. The butterflies may be seen in the wild from June till September, and the caterpillars (3), which live concealed in the grass, from autumn until May. The caterpillars hibernate and feed on various grasses.

The Dusky Meadow Brown (4) has a wingspan of 37—43 mm. The male resembles the Meadow Brown; the female is conspicuously different — she has two eyespots on the forewing. The butterflies of the single generation are on

4

1

2

3

5

the wing from June till August. The
caterpillar feeds on smooth
Meadow-grass and other grasses and
hibernates.

The Gatekeeper (5) has a wingspan of
30—38 mm. The female is larger and
paler than the male. The life habits and
development are the same as in the
preceding species.

93

Ringlet
Aphantopus hyperantus L.

Satyridae

The Ringlet is a typical inhabitant of open forests, forest margins, woodland clearings, and shrubby meadows with hedgerows of Blackberry bushes. In these biotopes it may be seen in abundance from June until late summer. The butterfly is not wary. It settles on all kinds of flowers as well as on the foliage of shrubs. The southern limit of its range in Europe is approximately the 42nd parallel. In the north it is distributed throughout all of Great Britain and Ireland except the extreme northern parts. In Finland and Scandinavia the northern limit of its range is approximately 62° latitude north. The Ringlet is mostly found in lowland district and at mid-altitudes. In mountains it generally does not occur above 1500 m.

The genus *Coenonympha* Hb. includes the smallest species of the family Satyridae. Europe is the home of 13 species. Of these the Small Heath (*Coenonympha pamphilus* L.) is the commonest and most widely distributed. It may be found in all kinds of grassy biotopes, where its modest requirements are easily satisfied. That is why it is relatively abundant also in cultivated countryside, in city parks and playgrounds, on grassy embankments and by roadsides. Its range is immense, embracing practically the whole of the western Palaearctic from northern Africa and Spain to Siberia. It does not do as well in mountain districts, even though it may be found at altitudes of as high as 2000 m.

6

5

The Ringlet has a wingspan of 35—42 mm. The male (1) is black-brown with indistinct eyespots on the upperside. The female (2) is larger and has a slightly paler hue, with black eyespots edged with orange. The underside of the wings is the same in both sexes (3). There is one generation a year, and the butterflies are on the wing from June till September.

94

2

1

4

3

The caterpillars may be found from autumn until May on various grasses.

The Small Heath (4) has a wingspan of 23—33 mm. The main difference between the male and female is in their size. The development of the caterpillars is relatively rapid and there are two or three generations a year; in cooler climates there is only one. The caterpillars (5) may be found throughout the year because the individual generations intermix. They feed on Rough Dog's Tail, meadow-grass, Annual Vernal Grass and other grasses. The pupa (6) with black stripes hangs by the cremaster on grasses. It is the caterpillar that hibernates.

Speckled Wood
Pararge aegeria L.

If you are out walking in a broad-leaved wood on a sunny spring day, you may see a colourful butterfly flitting in and out among the tree trunks and leafless branches. It is the Speckled Wood, distributed throughout a vast range extending from northern Africa through the whole of Europe to central Asia. Because it inhabits broad-leaved woods of mainly oak and beech, in Europe it occurs only as far up as 1000 m and in northern Africa up to 2000 m at the most. It is also interesting to note that the nominate form ssp. *aegeria* L., native to the southern parts of the range, as the pale expanses on the wings coloured orange, whereas in the ssp. *tircis* Butl. (= *egerides* Stgr.), which is found in central Europe, they are pale yellow. The Speckled Wood is fond of the partial shade of open, broad-leaved woods and is fairly abundant throughout its range, where it may be encountered from spring until autumn.

Another important woodland butterfly, exhibiting a preference for grassy, forest clearings, forest rides and woodland meadows, is the Large Wall Brown (*Lasiommata maera* L.). It, too, has a very large range, similar to that of the preceding species and extending in Asia to the Himalayas. In Europe it is not found in the British Isles and is absent also from the northwestern parts of the Continent and from some Mediterranean islands. In mountains it occurs up to 2000 m, where it flies in company with the very similar mountain species, the Northern Wall Brown (*L. petropolitana* F.). Like most satyrids the Large Wall Brown shows considerable variability in the wing markings.

The Speckled Wood (1) has a wingspan of 32—42 mm. There are regularly two generations a year, and in the south there may be even more. Depending on the arrival of spring the first generation is on the wing from March till June and the second from July till September. The

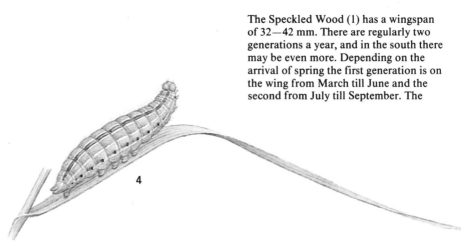

4

caterpillars, coloured green with a dark
dorsal stripe, feed, in late spring to early
summer and those of the second
generation in autumn, on fescue, brome,
meadow-grass and other grasses. It is the
pupa that hibernates.

The Large Wall Brown has a wingspan
of 37—50 mm. The male (2) is smaller
than the female (3), which also has more
prominent eyespots on the wings. There
are two generations a year; the first flies
in May and June and the second in
August and September. The caterpillar
(4), which feeds on various grasses,
hibernates and pupates in spring. The
pupa hangs by its hind end on grasses.

97

Wall Brown
Lasiommata megera L.

The Wall Brown has a very extensive range stretching from northern Africa through the whole of central and southern Europe all the way to central Asia. Compared with the range of other species of *Lasiommata* Westw., that of the Wall Brown is slightly more southerly excluding, as it does, northern Britain and, apart from the southernmost parts, Scandinavia. This is due to the fact that it is not a woodland species. It is mostly found on stony banks, in fields, on fallow land, bare loamy and gravelly banks, and sand dunes. It is fond of resting on the ground and even more so on milestones, walls, stones and rocks. The coloration of the underside of the wings is adapted to this background, and when it rests with closed wings the butterfly blends perfectly with its surroundings. The upperside of the wings is vividly coloured. The male's markings differ slightly from those of the female — there is a prominent, wide, black band of scent scales on the upperside of his forewings — and he is usually also smaller than the female. The ground colour of the female is paler.

The Wall Brown was described by Linné according to specimens from Austria and Denmark. The nominate form is distributed throughout all of Europe and, in areas with especially suitable conditions, occurs in relative abundance. It would seem that even the modern encroachments of civilization on the wilderness have not had any marked effect on its numbers. Found on the Mediterranean islands of Corsica and Sardinia is the slightly different ssp. *paramegaera* Hb.

The Wall Brown has a wingspan of 35—45 mm. There is marked sexual dichroism between the male (1) and female (2). However, the coloration of the underside of the wings is the same in both sexes (3). There are two generations a year; in the southern part of the range there may be as many as three. The first generation is on the wing in Europe from April to June, the second from July to

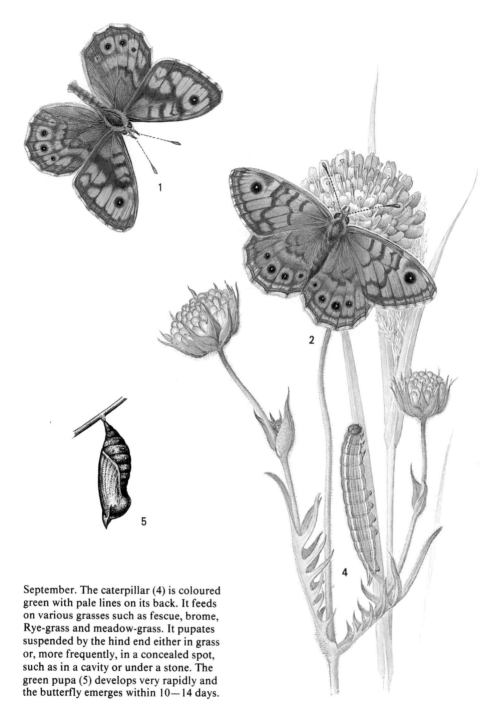

September. The caterpillar (4) is coloured green with pale lines on its back. It feeds on various grasses such as fescue, brome, Rye-grass and meadow-grass. It pupates suspended by the hind end either in grass or, more frequently, in a concealed spot, such as in a cavity or under a stone. The green pupa (5) develops very rapidly and the butterfly emerges within 10—14 days.

Duke of Burgundy Fritillary
Hamearis lucina L.

Riodinidae

The family of metalmarks is a small one with only about 1500 species described to date throughout the whole world. Most are found in tropical America. In recent years some authorities have voiced the opinion that this is merely a subfamily and that it belongs to the family of blues, coppers and hairstreaks (Lycaenidae).

The Duke of Burgundy Fritillary is the only species of this family in Europe. Its distribution extends from Spain through central and southern Europe to the central part of the Soviet Union. It is also found on the British Isles, in the Baltic republics of the USSR and in southern Sweden. It inhabits open, broad-leaved woods and shrubby countryside with plenty of flowering, uncultivated meadows. In the mountains it occurs up to altitudes of about 1300 m. In Europe it used to be a common butterfly but in recent years it has been declining markedly in number for no apparent reason. Perhaps it is affected by the general changes in the countryside caused primarily by the development of industry and agriculture.

The Nettle-tree Butterfly (*Libythea celtis* Laich.), also illustrated on the opposite page, is a member of another small family (the Snout Butterflies — Libytheidae). There are only some 20 species in the world and only one in Europe. This butterfly is found in the warm southern parts of Europe, whence in some years it flies to central Europe. It is distributed also from northern Africa through Asia Minor and Siberia to Japan. It is notable for the notched front wings, the long labial palps and the striking coloration.

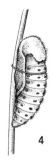

4

The Duke of Burgundy Fritillary (1) has a wingspan of 25—28 mm. A typical feature is the coloration on the underside of the wings (2). In the northern part of its range the butterflies are smaller and there is only one generation a year; in the south there are two. They are on the wing from April till June, in the south from as early as March with the second generation flying in August and September. The caterpillar (3) feeds from August on various primroses, occasionally also on other herbaceous plants. It hibernates and completes its development the following spring. The adult butterfly emerges from the pupa (4) after one to two weeks.

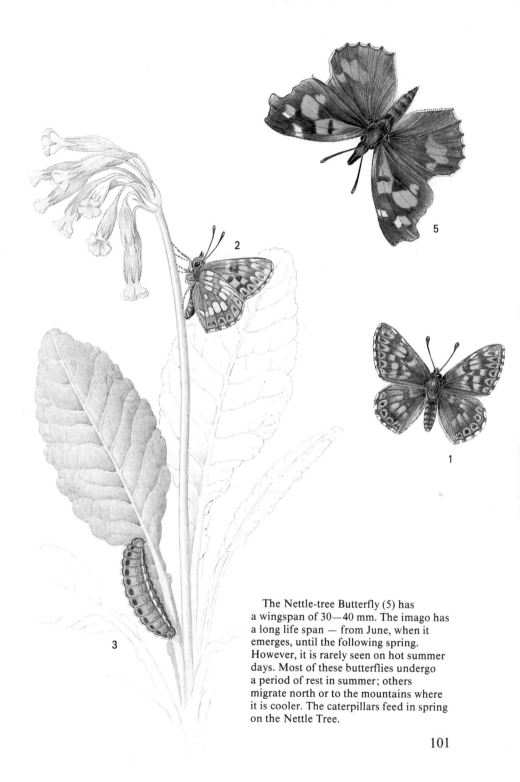

The Nettle-tree Butterfly (5) has a wingspan of 30—40 mm. The imago has a long life span — from June, when it emerges, until the following spring. However, it is rarely seen on hot summer days. Most of these butterflies undergo a period of rest in summer; others migrate north or to the mountains where it is cooler. The caterpillars feed in spring on the Nettle Tree.

Brown Hairstreak
Thecla betulae L.

Lycaenidae

The family Lycaenidae is a large one, embracing a great many species of small butterflies — more than 6000 worldwide. There are approximately 100 species that are native to Europe which makes this group of butterflies one of the largest on the Continent as well. The family is divided into three distinct subfamilies: the hairstreaks, coppers, and blues, to which the metalmarks (Riodinidae) are sometimes also added as a further subfamily.

The Brown Hairstreak is the largest and most striking of the European hairstreaks. It is found in the broad-leaved forest zone throughout practically the entire Palaearctic region — that is, excluding the extreme northern and extreme southern parts of Europe — and in Asia as far as Korea. It is a butterfly of lowland districts found only as high up as 1000 m. It has a preference for parkland with shrubs and thin woods, where it flies about in late summer and autumn. During the past decades, however, it has completely disappeared from many of its former habitats — apparently due to unacceptable environmental changes.

The Green Hairstreak (*Callophrys rubi* L.), distributed throughout the whole Palaearctic region, is a differently coloured type. In North America there are closely related species whose range at one time appeared to be linked with that of the Green Hairstreak. This wary butterfly is an agile flier and because of its sombre coloration readily escapes notice, even though it occurs in large numbers in shrubby localities, forest margins and moors.

The Brown Hairstreak has a wingspan of 32—37 mm. The male is nearly black without any markings on the upperside of the wings, whereas the female (1) has a conspicuous yellow patch on the forewings. The underside of the wings (2) of both sexes is yellow-orange. The caterpillars feed in spring on Blackthorn, plum trees, hazel and birch. The pupa is quiescent the whole summer. The butterflies of the one generation are on the wing from August till October. It is the egg that hibernates.

The Green Hairstreak (3) has a wingspan of 24—28 mm and the upperside of the wings is dark brown. There is no difference in the coloration of the male and female. The green colouring of the underside of the wings is a striking

5

feature. There are one or two generations, depending on climatic conditions. The first is on the wing from March till June, the second in August and September. The caterpillar (4) feeds on various plants, mostly Broom, clover and Bramble, and hibernates. The grey-brown pupa (5) makes a rattling sound when it moves.

Purple Hairstreak
Quercusia quercus L.

The Purple Hairstreak occurs in oak forests throughout Europe and in northern Africa. In the east it is distributed from the Near East to Transcaucasia. It is absent from northern Great Britain, Ireland and, with the exception of the warmest southern districts, practically the whole of Scandinavia. Neither does it occur high up in the mountains — 1500 m at the highest in the southern part of its range. It is found where the food plants of the caterpillar grow, i. e. various species of oak. This butterfly is still relatively abundant, but because it flies about in the tops of trees it often escapes notice. Adults are marked by sexual dichroism: the female has black wings with metallic blue patches, the male is a glossy grey.

Many hairstreaks of the genus *Strymonidia* Tutt and genus *Nordmannia* Tutt are very similar and can be distinguished only by the markings on the underside of the wings. One of these is the White-letter Haistreak (*Strymonidia w-album* Knoch). It is found in broad-leaved forests throughout practically all of Europe except southern Spain and the extreme northern regions, also in the east through all of Asia to Japan. Single specimens fly about in damp places in woods and in valleys alongside streams. They like to visit flowering Danewort, Hemp Agrimony, umbelliferous plants, and the like. In recent years this species has disappeared from many of its old localities. Its existence is apparently endangered by modern-day changes in its natural habitat, chiefly worldwide atmospheric pollution.

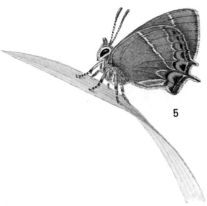

5

The Purple Hairstreak has a wingspan of 28—33 mm. Sexual dichroism is evident on the upperside of the wings (1 — female). The underside of the wings (2) is characteristic for this species. There is one generation a year, with the butterflies on the wing from June till August. The egg hibernates. The caterpillar (3) feeds from April till June on oaks. It pupates in a loose cocoon, between leaves that it has spun up. The pupa (4) is yellow-brown, short and rounded.

The White-letter Hairstreak (5) has a wingspan of 27—30 mm. The male and female are both dark brown without markings; the female is slightly paler. The markings on the underside of the wings are characteristic of the species. There is one generation a year, which is on the wing from June till August. The egg hibernates. The food plants of the caterpillar include elm, lime, willow and oak.

Scarce Copper
Heodes virgaureae L.

Lycaenidae

The ten species of coppers living in Europe may be likened to gems as far as butterflies go. Apart from a few exceptions, they glow with vivid colours and gleam in the sun so brightly that they catch one's eye despite their small dimensions. The Scarce Copper is the most plentiful of them all. It inhabits an extensive range embracing practically the whole of the Palaearctic region to Mongolia. In Europe it is absent from the northern parts of Scandinavia, the British Isles and the southernmost parts of the Mediterranean region. Its favourite haunts are meadows and forest margins, forest rides, and woodland clearings with lush vegetation. The butterfly likes resting on flowering agrimony, Groundsel and mint. It occurs in large numbers alongside streams. In mountains it is present at altitudes of up to 1500 m.

Very similar, even though it has entirely different requirements, is the Large Copper (*Lycaena dispar* Hw.). The male, unlike that of the preceding species, has a black spot on the upperside of the wings and the coloration of the underside is entirely different. This species has a scattered distribution in Europe and Asia as far as the Amur River. It inhabits damp meadows and in recent years has been disappearing as a result of land drainage; in many of its former habitats it has vanished completely. For example, the originally described, nominate form became extinct in England as early as the nineteenth century. Later the occurrence of the species was renewed there by the introduction of ssp. *batava* Oberth. from continental Europe. Central European populations belong to the subspecies *rutilus* Wernb.

4

The Scarce Copper has a wingspan of 27—32 mm. The male (1) is a fiery reddish brown; the female (2) has black dots on the wings and the greater part of the wings is coloured brown. Occasionally the females show a tendency towards melanism, i. e. entirely dark colouring. The underside of the wings is typical (3). There is one generation a year, with the butterflies on the wing from June till August. The caterpillar begins its development in

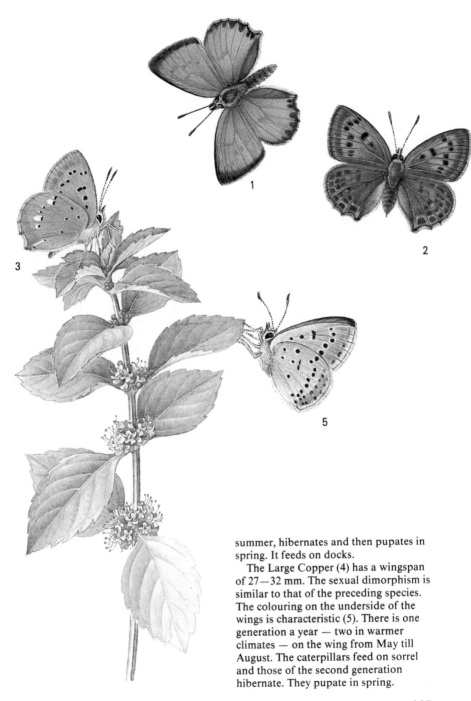

1

2

3

5

summer, hibernates and then pupates in spring. It feeds on docks.

The Large Copper (4) has a wingspan of 27—32 mm. The sexual dimorphism is similar to that of the preceding species. The colouring on the underside of the wings is characteristic (5). There is one generation a year — two in warmer climates — on the wing from May till August. The caterpillars feed on sorrel and those of the second generation hibernate. They pupate in spring.

Small Copper
Lycaena phlaeas L.

Lycaenidae

The Small Copper inhabits literally half the world: all of Europe and Asia to Japan, including various islands. Besides the part of Africa bordering the Mediterranean it is found also in Ethiopia and in North America, in the eastern United States and Canada. This distribution is undoubtedly due in great part to its powers of flight. This small butterfly is capable of migrating to new regions and making up for the losses suffered by the local or more extensive populations. In the mountains it may be found up to altitudes of 2000 m. Because of the mingling of populations this species did not develop any distinct geographic forms excepting ssp. *polaris* Courv., described from northern Europe and distinguished by the grey colouring of the underside of the hind wings. Otherwise this species exhibits marked individual variability. Its favourite haunts are rather dry, treeless localities. It often settles on the warm earth and basks in the sun. It is an extremely wary butterfly and a swift flier.

The Purple-edged Copper *(Palaeochrysophanus hippothoe)* has slightly different requirements. It occurs more to the north, throughout Europe and Asia to the Amur, and at mid to high altitudes, up to 2000 m. It is found in damp to boggy meadows. In drier districts and in the warm south its distribution is scantier. Its coloration is very variable; there are diverse tints in the sheen of the wings and it frequently produces even very dark individuals.

1

The Small Copper (1) has a wingspan of 22—27 mm. The male and female are similar, although the female is somewhat larger. There are one or two generations a year (depending on the climate and on the elevation), which overlap so that the butterflies may sometimes be seen from as early as February and, if the weather is warm, as late as October. The caterpillar (2) feeds on docks and hibernates. It pupates in spring (3).

The Purple-edged Copper has

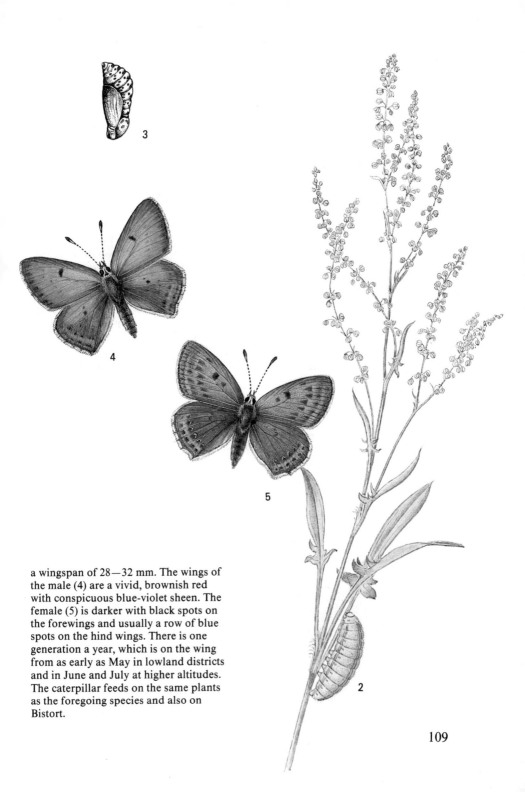

a wingspan of 28—32 mm. The wings of the male (4) are a vivid, brownish red with conspicuous blue-violet sheen. The female (5) is darker with black spots on the forewings and usually a row of blue spots on the hind wings. There is one generation a year, which is on the wing from as early as May in lowland districts and in June and July at higher altitudes. The caterpillar feeds on the same plants as the foregoing species and also on Bistort.

Large Blue
Maculinea arion L.

Lycaenidae

Of the approximately 70 species of blues found in Europe the Large Blue is the biggest. It occurs in the temperate regions of Europe and Asia, being absent only from the southernmost parts. Throughout its range it has a scattered, local distribution, occurring in dry, grassy places, in meadows and pastureland where there are small mounds of earth covered with Wild Thyme and inhabited by ants (e. g. the species *Tetramorium caespitum*). The reason for this is that the Large Blue, or rather the caterpillars, are dependent on ants. The young caterpillars feed on Wild Thyme, but older caterpillars live in the ant-hills and eat the larvae and pupae of their hosts. It is interesting to note that the ants do not harm these myrmecophilous caterpillars; on the contrary they tend them with care, for the caterpillars secrete drops of a special fluid that is an irresistible drug for the ants. The pupae likewise rest amongst the ants without harm until the emergence of the butterflies, which then leave the anthill. In recent years the Large Blue has become nearly or quite extinct in many localities and is one of the most endangered butterflies. The main reason is the ploughing up of meadows and pastureland and the intensive use of fertilizers and pesticides. As the ant colonies disappear so does this butterfly.

The Small Blue (*Cupido minimus* Fuessl.) is a dwarf in comparison with the other blues. It is only about half the size of the preceding species. Except for southern Spain, the Mediterranean islands and the extreme northern parts of Scandinavia, it inhabits all of Europe and Asia as far as the Amur. It is found in grassy places from lowland to mountain districts often as high as about 3000 m. In recent years this species also has disappeared from many areas, particularly from lowlands.

4

The Large Blue (1) has a wingspan of 28—38 mm. The underside of the wings is typical (2) and distinguishes it readily from other similar blues. The single generation is on the wing between May and August, depending on the altitude and climatic conditions. The caterpillar (3) feeds on Wild Thyme, then later on ant larvae and pupae inside an anthill, where it hibernates. The pupa lies inside the anthill for a brief period in spring.

The Small Blue (4, 5) has a wingspan of 18—22 mm. The female is dark brown; the male's wings have scattered blue scales, particularly at the base. There are two or three generations a year, depending on the climate, with butterflies on the wing from April till August. The caterpillar feeds in summer on coronilla, bird's-foot trefoil, Kidney Vetch and other leguminous plants.

Silver-studded Blue
Plebejus argus L.

Lycaenidae

Most blues exhibit sexual dichroism, which means that the male and female have different coloration. The male is generally a lovely blue colour, whereas the female is usually dark brown or, at most, has some orange spots near the edge of the wings. Such is the case with the Silver-studded Blue, one of the commonest blues in the wild. The butterflies flit about in dry as well as rather damp meadows. They congregate on the moist soil around drying puddles, and when disturbed they all fly up and away at the same time. They spend the night on blades of grass and in the early morning are often covered with minute drops of dew. The Silver-studded Blue is distributed throughout the entire Palaearctic region to Japan, except for northern Africa. In Europe it occurs only in the northernmost parts of the British Isles and in Scandinavia beyond the Arctic Circle.

The Chequered Blue (*Scolitantides orion* Pall.) has much more specific requirements. Although it is also distributed from Europe to Japan, in Europe its range is divided into two zones: the one a narrow belt through the southernmost parts of Finland and Scandinavia, separated by a gap from the main area of its distribution, which begins at 50° latitude north and extends southeastwards. To date, however, it has not been found in many areas in the western part of the Mediterranean region. This thermophilous blue is seen most often on rocky, sunny slopes where the food plants of the caterpillars grow.

The Silver-studded Blue has a wingspan of 20—23 mm. The male (1) is blue, the female (2) brown. There are orange spots near the edge of the underside of the wings (3).There are one or two generations a year, depending on the climate. The first generation is on the wing in May and June, the second in July and August. The myrmecophilous caterpillar feeds on coronilla, clover, Wild Thyme and other plants often growing on the nests of small ants such as *Tetramorium caespitum.*

4

The Chequered Blue (4) has a wingspan of 22—28 mm. The male and female are similar. This butterfly is readily distinguished from other blues by the underside of the wings (5). There are two generations a year. The first is on the wing in April and May, the second in July and August. The food plants of the myrmecophilous caterpillars are mostly Orpine and White Stonecrop. The pupae of the second generation hibernate.

3

5

1

2

Chalk-hill Blue
Lysandra coridon Poda

The Chalk-hill Blue is one of the larger blues. The male is greyish blue with darker veins on the wings. The outer part of the wings is brownish and the edge is rimmed with a long, white, dark-spotted fringe. The female is entirely brown, quite often dusted with blue. She has a small, black spot in the centre of the wings and is darker on the underside than the male. The Chalk-hill Blue's distribution is limited to Europe, mainly to the temperate regions. It is absent from all of Finland and Scandinavia as well as from Ireland. In Great Britain it occurs only in a relatively small area in the south; in Spain, on the other hand, it is only in the north. It is also absent from the north-western part of West Germany, from southern Italy, southern Greece and the Mediterranean islands. In other words the centre of its distribution is in central Europe, where it is found in dry, grassy localities and forest-steppes on sun-warmed banks, particularly ones with a limestone substrate. In biotopes not affected by man's activities it occurs in large numbers and in the middle of summer is one of the dominant species there. It is most abundant in lower-lying areas but may be encountered up to altitudes of 2000 m if the locality meets its ecological requirements.

Throughout Europe one will find the nominate form described from Austria. Only in central Spain is there an isolated subspecies, *saturiensis* Sag., which is slightly smaller and coloured a gleaming pale blue. The great variability of this species is influenced by the weather as well as habitat.

2

The Chalk-hill Blue has a wingspan of 30—35 mm. The male (1) is blue, the female (2) usually brown. They also differ in the colouring on the underside of the wings (3, 4), the female (fig. 4) being browner. There is generally only one generation a year. The butterflies are on the wing from June till August, but the greatest number is present in the second half of July. In warm years they may appear as early as May, and there may be a partial second generation by the end of

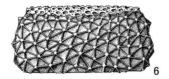

the summer (in the southern parts of its range). The caterpillar (5) is myrmecophilous. It feeds on vetches, coronilla, and other leguminous plants. It hibernates and pupates in spring. The pupal stage is very brief. The egg (6) is shaped like a low, flattened cylinder and has a typical textured surface.

Common Blue
Polyommatus icarus Rott.

This species is one of the commonest and most widely distributed of the blues. It inhabits the Palaearctic region from northern Africa and southwestern Europe through all of Asia to the Far East and the Pacific Ocean. It has also settled in the far north beyond the Arctic Circle and may be found in mountains up to even 3000 m. This suggests a very great ecological adaptability, which is probably the reason why it is one of the few butterflies that has adapted successfully to the changes brought about by civilization. It is even found in intensively cultivated fields. Perhaps this also has to do with the fact that the caterpillars feed on Lucerne, which is cultivated for fodder and hence is not treated with insecticides. The Common Blue inhabits forestless countryside, occuring in large numbers in steppes and in rather dry meadows together with the Small Tortoiseshell, whites, fritillaries and other blues. All of these may be seen on puddles and on damp sand beside streams, where they drink water. The typical coloration of the males is blue-violet.

The Adonis Blue (*Lysandra bellargus* Rott.), which has azure blue wings edged with black and white chequered fringes, is distributed in the warmer parts of Europe. In the east its range extends to Iraq and Iran. It may be seen on the wing mostly in lowland districts; in mountain districts it is found only in the warmer ranges, and no higher than 2000 m.

5

The Common Blue has a wingspan of 25—30 mm. There is marked sexual dichroism between the blue male (1) and brown female (2). Characteristic of the species is the underside of the wings (3). There are one to three overlapping generations a year, depending on the climate. Sometimes butterflies are on the wing from as early as April and until September. The caterpillars (4) feed on restharrows, bird's foot trefoils, Lucerne, clovers, and similar plants; those of the last generation hibernate. In May the caterpillar changes into a green pupa (5), from which the butterfly emerges shortly after.

2

1

3

6

4

The Adonis Blue has a wingspan of
27—32 mm. Again, the male (6) is blue,
the female brown. There are two
generations a year; the first is on the wing
in May and June, the second in August
and September. The caterpillar
hibernates. The food plants include
clover, Genista, bird's-foot trefoil and
Horseshoe Vetch.

Grizzled Skipper
Pyrgus malvae L.

Hesperiidae

Although traditionally the skippers are often classified as butterflies, in actual fact they form a group that is far removed from butterflies and is anatomically closest to the pyralids. The only characteristics reminiscent of butterflies are their consistent diurnal activity and the stiff antennae enlarged at the tip. On the other hand the venation, head, massive thorax and the shape of the caterpillar's body are entirely different. Throughout the world there are some 4000 species of skippers. Most are native to South America, where the genetic centre of this family is located. Only about 40 species are found in Europe.

The Grizzled Skipper is one of the most common skippers. It belongs to a genus that comprises a full third of the European species of this family. With the exception of the coldest parts of Scandinavia it occurs practically everywhere in Europe in dry, grassy places, in hedgerows, on grassy banks and on forest rides. In the east its range extends through the temperate regions of Asia to Mongolia. It is a butterfly of early spring and is fond of settling on flowering Tormentil, Wild Strawberry, Bugle and the like. However, it is extremely wary.

The Mallow Skipper (*Carcharodus alceae* Esp.) also is on the wing early in spring. It is a thermophilous species and its centre of distribution is in southern Europe. Because the northern limit of its range is at about 52° north it is not found in England, Denmark, Finland or Scandinavia, and in the northern parts of Germany is encountered only on the rare occasion.

4

The Grizzled Skipper (1) has a wingspan of 18—22 mm. It is best distinguished from other similar species by the markings on the underside of the wings (2). There are two generations a year, which are on the wing from April till August. The caterpillar feeds on the Wild Strawberry or the Tormentil, and it completes its development in the autumn. The pupa hibernates.

The Mallow Skipper (3) has a wingspan of 23—30 mm and is thus one of the larger species. The female has the same coloration as the male but may be somewhat larger. There are two or three generations a year; butterflies of the first are on the wing in spring from March till May, those of the other generations

overlap and are on the wing from July till September. The caterpillars (4) live on and hibernate in spun-up leaves of the Common Mallow and Marsh Mallow. The pupa (5) may be found in early spring, likewise in spun-up leaves.

Chequered Skipper
Carterocephalus palaemon Pall.

Hesperiidae

The range of this strikingly coloured butterfly embraces practically all of Europe, central and northern Asia and North America with the exception of the warmest parts of the Mediterranean region. It is absent, for example, from Italy, Spain and Greece. An inhabitant of the broad-leaved forests of the temperate zone, it is particularly fond of thin woods with thick herbaceous undergrowth and grassy, flowering enclaves. In most of Europe it was formerly quite common in forests, but in recent decades its numbers have been rapidly declining for no apparent reason. In many parts of western Europe it is already considered an endangered species. In central Europe, although it is still quite plentiful, its numbers have declined greatly in comparison with former times. The reason may be global changes in the biosphere, in some places changes in forestry practice, in the technology of logging and reafforestation and in the composition of forest stands.

The Small Skipper (*Thymelicus sylvestris* Poda) is the most common and most widespread of four similar species. The Essex, or European Skipper (*T. lineola* O.) is also well known. The Small Skipper's range extends from northern Africa through all of Europe (except Ireland, Finland and Scandinavia) to the Middle East as far as Iran. It is a woodland species and the butterfly may be seen flying on forest rides, on shrubby banks and in forest margins, or resting on flowering Field Scabious, Cornflower and thistles. It is most plentiful at lowland and mid-altitudes, and in mountains may be present up to 2000 m. It exhibits marked variability in coloration.

4

The Chequered Skipper (1, 2) has a wingspan of 22—28 mm. The dark pattern is variable; the yellow spots are sometimes greatly reduced. The coloration on the underside of the wings (3) is a characteristic feature of this species. There is one generation a year, with the butterflies on the wing from May till June and, at higher altitudes, also in July. The caterpillar (4) appears in autumn, hibernates and completes its development in spring. It feeds primarily on plantains, otherwise also on some grasses.

The Small Skipper has a wingspan of 24—27 mm. The male (5) differs from the female by having a dark, oblique band of scent scales. Characteristic of this skipper also is the underside of the wings (6). The butterflies of the single generation are on the wing from June till August. The caterpillar feeds on various grasses, spinning the blades together to form a chamber in which it rests. It hibernates and then pupates in spring.

Large Skipper
Ochlodes venatus Bremer et Grey.

Hesperiidae

The Large Skipper was described in 1857 according to a specimen from China. The populations inhabiting central Europe are included in ssp. *septentrionalis* Verity. China, however, does not mark the limit of the species' range, which extends as far as Japan. It includes the entire Palaearctic region with the exception of northern Africa, southern Spain, several Mediterranean islands, Ireland, Scotland and the northern parts of Scandinavia beyond the Arctic Circle. It is a common butterfly of forested as well as forestless country and may be encountered everywhere on shrubby banks, forest rides, and in forest clearings as well as in hedgerows between fields from lowland to mountain districts up to altitudes of 2000 m.

The Silver-spotted Skipper (*Hesperia comma* L.) is very similar but can be distinguished from the preceding species by the undersides of the wings, which have prominent white spots. The slanting, black patch of scent scales on the forewings of the male is divided lengthwise into two parts by a whitish line. This species has an even greater area of distribution than the former. It is found also in northern Africa, northern Norway and North America and in Asia occurs throughout the temperate zone. It is one of the commonest butterflies in thin woods and shrubby, as well as grassy, biotopes; it is not uncommon either at the edges of fields and in city parks. In mountains it occurs up to 2500 m. It prefers limestone substrates but is by no means restricted to these.

3

The Large Skipper has a wingspan of 25—32 mm. The male (1) differs from the female (2) in the pattern and coloration of the wings. There is one generation a year with the butterflies flying about from June till August. The green caterpillar, with a dark stripe down its back and yellow stripe on either side, lives in autumn on various grasses, e. g. meadow-grass, Common Couch, oat-grass and Soft Grass. Then it hibernates and in spring changes into a slender, greenish yellow pupa.

The Silver-spotted Skipper has
a wingspan of 25—30 mm. The male (3)
has a patch of scent scales on each
forewing; the female (4) has no such
patches. There is one generation a year,
which is on the wing from June till
September. The caterpillar (5) lives from
autumn until spring close to the ground
inside a tube of grass stems and blades
spun together. Its food plants are fescue,
meadow-grass and Common Couch as
well as coronilla, bird's-foot trefoil etc.
The slender, brown pupa may be found
in May on the ground in a loose cocoon.

Garden Tiger
Arctia caja L.

Arctiidae

The family of tiger and footman moths numbers some 8000 species distributed throughout the world but primarily in South America. Only about 80 species are found in Europe. Of these the Garden Tiger is undoubtedly the best known. Besides Europe and Asia it is distributed also in North America. It occurs from lowland districts to altitudes of around 2000 m. However, it thrives best in foothills about 600 m above sea level, where it is very abundant in many places. Despite this it is not easily spotted for it remains concealed in vegetation during the daytime and ventures out only at night. Specimens may be obtained, however, by rearing them from the large, hairy caterpillars collected in spring with little difficulty for they are quite plentiful in the wild. They are extremely voracious and develop rapidly. They generally pupate in a cocoon close to the ground.

The Cream-spot Tiger (*Arctia villica* L.) is a thermophilous species distributed in the warmer parts of Europe and Asia, its range extending approximately to Transcaucasia. The pattern of the wings is, as in the preceding species, very variable, and a great many individual forms have been described, many of them very extreme. One example is f. *paucimacula*, in which the pale markings on the forewings tend to disappear completely so that the moth is practically all brown.

The Garden Tiger (1) has a wingspan of 45—65 mm. The male has pectinate antennae and is usually smaller than the female, which has a very stout abdomen. There is one generation a year. The moths are on the wing in July and August. The mouthparts are rudimentary so the moths do not feed. The caterpillar (2), which is polyphagous, hibernates when partly developed and completes its development in spring. The hairs (3) have short lateral projections. The plump, black pupa (4) is encased in a cocoon that also contains hairs from the caterpillar.

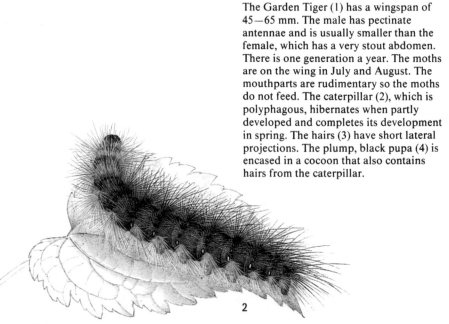

2

The Cream-spot Tiger (5) has a wingspan of 45—60 mm. The differences between the male and female are similar to those of the preceding species as is the life cycle: there is one generation a year and a polyphagous caterpillar that hibernates when partly developed and pupates immediately in spring. The moths are on the wing in May and June.

Scarlet Tiger
Panaxia dominula L.

Arctiidae

This handsome moth is distributed only in Europe, its range extending to the Caucasus. It inhabits damp forests and valleys with lush vegetation from lowland to mountain districts, up to 2500 m. Together with the following species it is one of the few tiger moths that has well-developed mouthparts and is hence capable of feeding. It may be found on flowers as well as on damp ground where it sucks water. Because it is capable of feeding it has a longer lifespan than moths that are dependent only on the body fat stored up by the caterpillar. The Scarlet Tiger is on the wing both during the day and at night and is extremely wary. It is most likely to be seen when it is suddenly disturbed and flies up from its hiding place. It exhibits marked variability in the arrangement of the spots on the forewings and hind wings. The metallic sheen on the dark parts of the forewing also varies and may have a green, blue or violet tinge. An unusual deviant is the form *flavia* with yellow hind wings. Some forms occur more frequently in certain districts and are sometimes classified as geographic races. One example is ssp. *pompalis* Nitsche, which inhabits southern Alpine valleys and has a more complex dark pattern on the wings.

The Jersey Tiger (*Euplagia quadripunctaria* Poda) has a more southerly range than that of the preceding species. Nevertheless, it may be found even high up in the mountains, although it prefers forest-steppe regions and rocky valleys with lush vegetation growing in moist places. It is on the wing mainly in the daytime.

The Scarlet Tiger (1) has a wingspan of 45—55 mm. There is no difference between the sexes; both have filiform antennae. The moths of the single generation are on the wing from May till July. The small caterpillar hibernates, completing its development (2) the following spring. It feeds on Stinging Nettle, dead-nettle, Raspberry and other plants. The pupa (3) is black and enclosed in a cocoon. The adult moth emerges after two to three weeks.

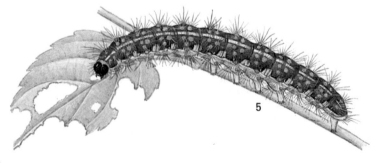

5

The Jersey Tiger (4) has a wingspan of 42—52 mm. The male and female are alike. There is a single generation a year, which is on the wing from July till September. The young caterpillars hibernate. The fully grown caterpillars (5) are brightly coloured and are polyphagous. The pupae differ only slightly from those of the preceding species.

127

Ammobiota festiva Hb. Arctiidae

This moth, better known by the synonym *Arctia hebe* L., is a thermophilous species. Although its distribution extends eastwards to northeastern China, it is found only in the warmer parts of Europe and Asia. It is very plentiful in the Mediterranean region, for example, whereas in central Europe it has a local distribution, occurring only in very warm habitats. It is a steppe and forest-steppe species, partial to sun-warmed, sandy or limestone substrates. Like most tiger moths it is very variable in its coloration. In southern Europe the moths are a more vivid red and black, whereas in central Europe they are grey and pink. This moth is highly prized by collectors for it is very difficult to obtain a specimen in the wild. It is best to collect the caterpillars after hibernation because a great many die during the winter.

Hyphoraia aulica L., another extremely variable tiger moth, is distributed throughout all of Europe and Asia to the Far East. However, nowhere does it occur in large numbers. It is found in warm biotopes with abundant vegetation. The caterpillars of a single brood do not develop at the same rate, and so it happens that the more rapidly developing individuals form a second generation the same year, while the others await the onset of hibernation in a partially developed state.

Ammobiota festiva Hb. (1) has a wingspan of 46—60 mm. The male has pectinate antennae. There is one generation a year, with the moths on the wing in May. The caterpillar (2) changes shortly after hibernation into a black pupa that has two clumps of stiff bristles terminating in discs on the cremaster (3). The caterpillars are polyphagous and like basking in the sun in spring. This moth

5

3

1

4

2

has become extinct in many areas and is an endangered species in central Europe.

Hyphoraia aulica L. (4) has a wingspan of 30—38 mm. There are one or two generations a year, depending on the climate and the weather. As a rule there is one generation on the wing in August. The caterpillar (5) has long hairs on its hind end. It is polyphagous and pupates in spring after hibernating.

Wood Tiger
Parasemia plantaginis L.

Arctiidae

The Wood Tiger is a smaller, but very interesting species, widely distributed throughout Europe and Asia as far as Japan. It may be found in lowland districts but is generally encountered in mountains where it commonly occurs even as high up as 3000 m. Only few moths exhibit such great variability in coloration. In this species hereditary forms combine with individual deviants produced by sudden changes of weather, and so the ground colour of the wings (different in the cases of males and females) may be anything from carmine-red to orange to pale yellow to white. The black markings on the wings either cover them almost completely so that there are only thin bands of the light colour or are reduced to merely a few patches by the outer edges of the hind wings. The females exhibit fewer variations and their hind wings are usually carmine-red. Males of the typical form with yellow hind wings occur only in lowland districts. In mountain districts the ground colour of the males' wings is more or less white (f. *hospita* and f. *bicolor*). The moths fly during the day as well as at night.

The Ruby Tiger (*Phragmatobia fuliginosa* L.) is a very common species. Its range embraces the entire Palaearctic region from northern Africa to Japan. The moths are attracted to light.

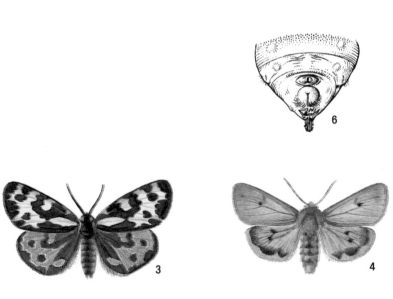

6

3

4

The Wood Tiger has a wingspan of 32—38 mm. It exhibits marked sexual dimorphism (the male has pectinate antennae) as well as ecologically influenced polychroism. The typically coloured male (1) has yellowish hind wings, whereas in mountain forms (2) the ground colour of the male's wings is white. The typical female (3) has red hind wings. The moths of the single generation are on the wing from May till August. The caterpillar is polyphagous. It hibernates when half-grown and pupates in spring in a brown cocoon.

The Ruby Tiger (4) has a wingspan of 30—35 mm. The male and female are alike. There are regularly two generations a year, the first being on the wing from April till June and the second from July till September. The caterpillar (5) feeds on various plants and only hibernates when it is fully grown. The dark brown pupa with yellow-edged abdominal segments has a tuft of hooked processes (6) on the cremaster.

131

White Ermine
Spilosoma lubricipeda L.

Arctiidae

The tiger and footman moths include in their number several white or nearly white species, some of which are very similar. One of the most common is the White Ermine, which is widespread in the whole of non-polar Europe and Asia and found in both lowland and mountain districts. On warm May evenings it often flies through an open window into a lighted room or in the morning may be found resting on a wall where a street lamp casts its light during the night.

The female Buff Ermine (*Spilosoma luteum* Hb.) is yellowish white, the male creamy yellow. This species is also widespread throughout Europe and Asia, but is slightly more thermophilous. It is found mainly in lowland districts, its numbers decreasing with increasing altitude up to 1000 m, above which limit it is no longer to be seen. It frequents parkland, fields, gardens and the vicinity of brooks and streams.

The Fall Webworm (*Hyphantria cunea* Drury) was introduced from North America to Hungary at the beginning of the Second World War. From there it spread to all the warm regions of central Europe and has become a serious pest of fruit trees and broad-leaved forest trees.

White-coloured species also include *Spilosoma urticae* Esp., which is very similar to the White Ermine, and the female of *Cycnia mendica* Cl., whose opposite sex (the male) is coloured brown. The males of all the foregoing species have pectinate (comb-like) antennae, whereas the females have setaceous (bristle-like) antennae.

The White Ermine (1) has a wingspan of 30—42 mm. There is one generation a year. The moths are on the wing from May to August. The caterpillar (2) is polyphagous and develops during the summer. It is the pupa that hibernates.

The Buff Ermine (3) has a wingspan of 28—40 mm. The moths of the single

4

3

generation are on the wing also from May to August. The hairy caterpillar (4) is paler than that of the preceding species. The pupa hibernates.

The Fall Webworm (5), with a wingspan of 25—40 mm, is the smallest of these three species. There are two generations a year. The first is on the wing from April to June, the second in late summer. The caterpillars (6) of the second generation complete their development in the autumn. The pupae hibernate in various hiding places and crevices.

133

Cinnabar Moth
Tyria jacobaeae L.

This is a very strikingly coloured moth with forewings black with red spots and red hind wings. There is no other like it in the whole tiger moth family. It is distributed throughout all of Europe and Asia Minor with central Asia marking the limit of its range. In mountains it occurs up to altitudes of about 1600 m. It is more plentiful, however, in lowland districts, where it may be found in grassy biotopes, hedgerows, rather dry meadows and in steppe and forest-steppe regions. Unfortunately it has declined markedly in number during the past decades due to the cultivation of meadows and nowadays is seen only here and there.

The genus *Eilema* Hb. includes approximately ten very similar species. One of the most abundant is the Scarce Footman (*Eilema complana* L.), which is distributed in the temperate regions of Europe eastwards as far as Transcaucasia. It may be encountered in warm, broad-leaved forests as well as in city parks and gardens. The modest caterpillars of these species feed on lichens and may be found together with their food plants not only on tree trunks but also on the ground and on rocks.

Interesting species of arctiids are those with narrow forewings and broad hind wings. One such is the Feathered Footman (*Spiris striata* L.), which inhabits all of Europe and Asia Minor. It is found in rather warm, grassy biotopes.

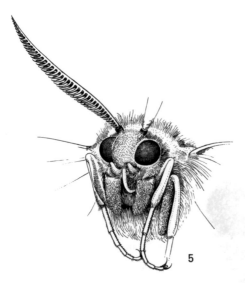

The Cinnabar Moth (1) has a wingspan of 32—42 mm. There is one generation a year, with the moths flying about from May till July. The caterpillars (2) live communally. They feed on Tansy, Ragwort and Groundsel. The pupa hibernates on the ground in a loose cocoon among spun-up leaves.

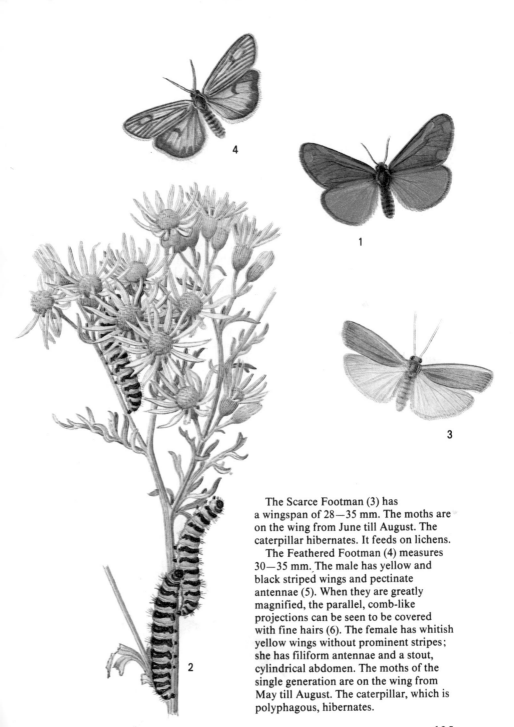

The Scarce Footman (3) has a wingspan of 28—35 mm. The moths are on the wing from June till August. The caterpillar hibernates. It feeds on lichens.

The Feathered Footman (4) measures 30—35 mm. The male has yellow and black striped wings and pectinate antennae (5). When they are greatly magnified, the parallel, comb-like projections can be seen to be covered with fine hairs (6). The female has whitish yellow wings without prominent stripes; she has filiform antennae and a stout, cylindrical abdomen. The moths of the single generation are on the wing from May till August. The caterpillar, which is polyphagous, hibernates.

Gipsy Moth
Lymantria dispar L.

Of the 1800 species of tussock moths distributed throughout the world, only 17 are found in Europe; the others are mostly indigenous to South America. However, even among the few European species there are some that are pests in horticulture and forestry.

The Gipsy Moth is a dangerous pest of broad-leaved trees. The hairy, brightly coloured caterpillars cause serious damage in oak woods by stripping the trees of their foliage. They also damage orchards and avenues of plum, apricot, walnut and other trees. This species is nowadays distributed throughout the northern hemisphere. In 1869 it was taken from Europe to North America for experimental purposes but escaped from captivity and established itself in the wild, becoming an even greater pest there than in its native land.

Another feared species is the Black Arches Moth (*Lymantria monacha* L.). It is widespread throughout the temperate zone of Europe and Asia, occurring, in comparison with the Gipsy Moth, more to the north and at higher elevations. It was in Europe's lowland districts, however, that it caused catastrophic damage at the beginning of this century when it multiplied in spruce monocultures that had been unsuitably planted there. Spruce is not the only food plant of the Black Arches Moth. The caterpillars feed on many other trees and that is why the moth occurs in relative abundance even in broad-leaved forests. In industrial regions it occurs in various dark to entirely black forms.

The Gipsy Moth has a wingspan of 32—55 mm. The male (1) is small and brown and has pectinate antennae. The female (2) is creamy white with brownish vermiculation, slender antennae and stout abdomen. There is one generation a year, and the moths are on the wing

3

136

from June till August. The eggs hibernate. The polyphagous caterpillars (3) are fully grown in late spring when they change into slightly hairy pupae.

1

2

4

The Black Arches Moth (4) has a wingspan of 30—50 mm. The male and female differ primarily in the shape of the antennae, the abdomen and size. The development is similar to that of the Gipsy Moth: the eggs hibernate and the caterpillar feeds in spring and pupates in May and June. The moths are on the wing at night from July till September. The food plants of the caterpillars are chiefly spruce and pine, but also oak and beech.

137

Pale Tussock Moth
Dasychira pudibunda L.

Lymantriidae

This common moth is found in broad-leaved forests throughout Europe and Asia as far as Japan. It also thrives in city parks and gardens and thus is common also in urban areas. Its vertical distribution, however, is limited to the upper limit of the broad-leaved forest. The coloration of the moths is very variable. There is a grey form, *concolor*, that is often seen in industrial districts.

Another member of the same family is the Vapourer (*Orgyia antiqua* L.), a small moth that inhabits broad-leaved and mixed forests in the northern and temperate regions of the Palaearctic. It is absent only from the warmest regions. Because the caterpillars are extremely polyphagous, this species is able to live even above the forest line, at altitudes of about 2000 m. Here the caterpillars feed on Bilberry, Dwarf Birch, willows and the like. This moth exhibits marked sexual dimorphism. The male is slender with pectinate antennae and flies in a darting fashion in the afternoon on warm, sunny days as well as at night. The female has only vestigial wings and weak legs with which she is barely able to crawl — in fact she practically makes no attempt to do so. After emerging from the pupa she remains beside her pupal cocoon where she is soon fertilized by the male and where she lays her whole batch of eggs. The dispersal of the species falls to the youngest caterpillars, as is usually the case with many species of tussock moths. Because they have long hairs they are readily blown by the wind throughout the surrounding countryside.

The Pale Tussock Moth has a wingspan of 40—65 mm. The male (1) is smaller, darker and has pectinate antennae. The female is stout, whitish and has filiform antennae. There is one generation a year, on the wing in May and June, and very occasionally a partial second generation, on the wing in August and September.

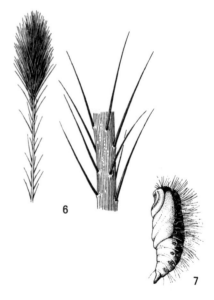

6

4

7

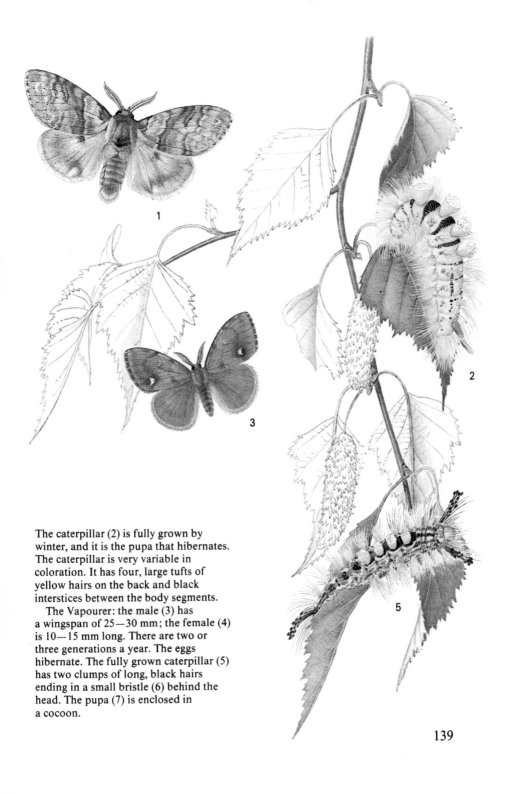

The caterpillar (2) is fully grown by winter, and it is the pupa that hibernates. The caterpillar is very variable in coloration. It has four, large tufts of yellow hairs on the back and black interstices between the body segments.

The Vapourer: the male (3) has a wingspan of 25—30 mm; the female (4) is 10—15 mm long. There are two or three generations a year. The eggs hibernate. The fully grown caterpillar (5) has two clumps of long, black hairs ending in a small bristle (6) behind the head. The pupa (7) is enclosed in a cocoon.

Turnip Moth
Agrotis segetum Den. et Schiff.

Noctuidae

The noctuids are the largest family of butterflies and moths, numbering more than 20 000 species worldwide. Of these more than 1100 species belong to the fauna of Europe. The noctuids are moreover considered to form one of the most advanced groups of Lepidoptera phylogenetically. This is because of such factors as their anatomy, morphology, and unusual ecological reactions (e. g. types of diapause).

The Turnip Moth was originally a steppe species that was widespread in the steppe areas of Europe and Asia. However, it moved to so-called cultivated steppe and adapted extremely well to life on cultivated agricultural tracts. Its reproductive ability, the polyphagous character of the caterpillars and its adaptability to varied conditions soon made it a feared pest, which, in years when it reached plague numbers, caused damage to crops on millions of hectares. The coloration of this moth is very variable, particularly in the case of the males, which range from pale to completely dark.

The Heart and Dart (*Agrotis exclamationis* L.) is also one of the most common moths in the temperate and warm parts of the entire Palaearctic. Interestingly, however, this species is not a destructive agricultural pest in spite of its great abundance. This is perhaps due in part to the slow development of the caterpillars and the extended occurrence of the usually one, single generation. The Heart and Dart prefers to feed on wild plants and in cultivated countryside occurs chiefly on the uncultivated areas.

The Turnip Moth has a wingspan of 27—40 mm. The male (1) has pectinate antennae and nearly white hind wings. The female (2) has filiform antennae and is a darker colour in general with greyish brown to whitish hind wings. There are one or two generations a year in central Europe; in warmer areas there may also

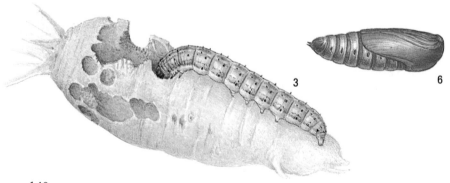

3

6

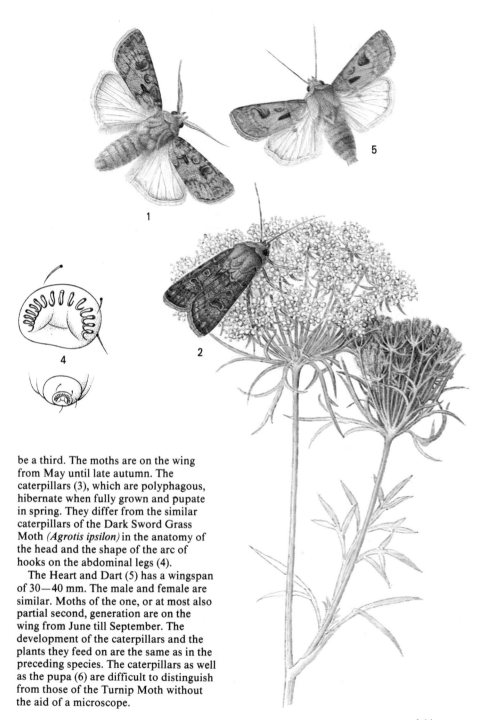

be a third. The moths are on the wing from May until late autumn. The caterpillars (3), which are polyphagous, hibernate when fully grown and pupate in spring. They differ from the similar caterpillars of the Dark Sword Grass Moth *(Agrotis ipsilon)* in the anatomy of the head and the shape of the arc of hooks on the abdominal legs (4).

The Heart and Dart (5) has a wingspan of 30—40 mm. The male and female are similar. Moths of the one, or at most also partial second, generation are on the wing from June till September. The development of the caterpillars and the plants they feed on are the same as in the preceding species. The caterpillars as well as the pupa (6) are difficult to distinguish from those of the Turnip Moth without the aid of a microscope.

141

Large Yellow Underwing
Noctua pronuba L.

Noctuidae

Of the members of the subfamily Noctuinae some ten have yellow hind wings. The most common and the largest is the Large Yellow Underwing, which is distributed throughout the whole Palaearctic except the far northern regions. In mountains it is commonly encountered up to altitudes of 2000 m, although one cannot exclude the possibility that such moths may have wandered there from lowland districts. This species has as exceptionally long flight period — from June until the autumn. It was long believed that there were two generations. However it was proved that the moths belonged to a single generation that aestivated (i.e. passed the summer in a state of dormancy) and did not begin multiplying — ovipositing — until late summer. The Large Yellow Underwing is a nocturnal moth, foraging for food in the evening and then flying about the countryside. It is attracted to bright lights in the period from shortly before midnight until morning.

The Broad-bordered Yellow Underwing (*Noctua fimbriata* Schreb.) is one of the most handsome moths with the contrasting coloration of the hind wings and wide range of hues of the forewings. It is found chiefly in central and southern Europe, its numbers diminishing towards the north; the Caucasus is the approximate eastern limit of its range. Its life history, like that of other members of the genus *Noctua*, is similar to that of the Large Yellow Underwing. The moths are on the wing from June, but eggs do not start developing in the females' ovaries until there is less than 15 hours of daylight, and so they are not deposited until August and September.

The Large Yellow Underwing has a wingspan of 45—65 mm. The male (1) has dark forewings, those of the female (2) are paler. There is one generation a year. The caterpillar (3) is polyphagous and is sometimes a pest in vegetable gardens. It hibernates when fully grown. In spring it feeds only briefly, and in May it pupates on the ground. The pupa (4) is a glossy yellow-brown. The cremaster (5) has two spines.

6

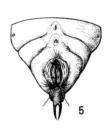

5

The Broad-bordered Yellow Underwing has a wingspan of 45—55 mm. The forewings of the male (6) are dark with a greenish or brownish red tinge, those of the female are straw-coloured. The caterpillar is polyphagous. It hibernates when half-grown, about 20 mm long. In spring, when it completes its development, it feeds at night on the buds and young leaves of various shrubs such as Blackthorn, Dog Rose and Privet.

143

Cabbage Moth
Mamestra brassicae L.

Noctuidae

The Cabbage Moth is distributed throughout the entire Palaearctic region, from Europe to Japan, and occurs also in North America. Though most abundant in lowland districts it may also be found in mountains at altitudes of approximately 2000 m. These specimens, however, are usually offspring of the first generation from lower elevations that fly into the mountains when spring begins there. This common moth is not noted for its beauty. It is one of the few species that often causes catastrophic damage in agriculture, especially to vegetables. When the caterpillars are present in vast numbers, they strip the plants bare, right down to the leaf stalk. Caterpillars of the autumn generation bore inside heads of cabbages, soil them with their watery excrement and make it impossible to store and process them further for such infested cabbages tend to spoil very rapidly. Whole research teams are trying to find ways to prevent such damage.

The Dot (*Mamestra persicariae* L.) is likewise distributed throughout the entire Palaearctic — in the temperate zone. It chooses open habitats, where it feeds on field crops as well as on plants growing in the wild. However, it is not a species that regularly reaches plague numbers. It is not variable in coloration. The only deviants are individuals that have the kidney-shaped spot on the forewings coloured brownish red (f. *accipitrina*) or black (f. *unicolor*).

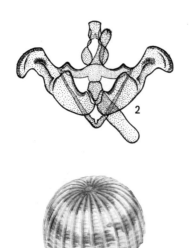

The Cabbage Moth (1) has a wingspan of 37—45 mm. The male and female differ only in anatomical features (2 — copulatory organs of the male). In cool climates there is only one generation a year, but in warmer climates there are two or three. Adult moths are on the wing without interruption from May to October, so the individual generations overlap. The caterpillar (3) is polyphagous but is partial to cruciferous plants. The yellow-brown pupa hibernates on the ground.

The Dot (4) has a wingspan of 37—40 mm. There is one generation a year, on the wing from May to August. The ribbed eggs (5) are pale green and are generally laid in a large cluster. The caterpillar (6) is polyphagous, greenish or brown, and with the eighth abdominal segment slightly raised. The black pupa hibernates in the ground in an earthen chamber. It has a typical cremaster (7) at the hind end.

Common Wainscot
Mythimna pallens L.

Noctuidae

This plain moth is distributed in the whole of Europe, Asia and in North America. It occurs in large numbers in dry steppe meadows as well as damp ones. It is less abundant as the altitude increases and higher up is replaced in ever greater numbers by the similar moth *M. impura* Hb. The whole group of moths that comprises the genus *Mythimna* O. prefers grasses. Some species are damp-loving and live inside the stems of reeds and other aquatic grasses, sedges etc., others live in turf in drier biotopes. In terms of coloration the moths have a number of common characteristics.

The several tens of species comprising the genus *Cucullia* Schr., apart from a few exceptions such as *C. argentea* Hfn., are quite plain. They are a monotonous grey or brown colour and it is often quite difficult to distinguish between them. The caterpillars, on the other hand, are brightly coloured and of varied shape. Collecting the caterpillars and raising the moths in captivity is a reliable way of obtaining specimens of a given species. The caterpillars may have cryptic (protective) or warning coloration. The Scarce Wormwood (*Cucullia artemisiae* Hfn.) is an example of perfect cryptic coloration and mimicry. Its caterpillar is indistinguishable from flowering Mugwort. The caterpillars of the Mullein (*Cucullia verbasci* L.) are excellently concealed when they move about among the flowers of mullein but when resting on the rosette of green leaves their coloration becomes warning coloration.

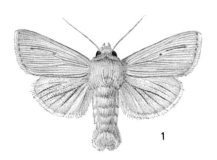

The Common Wainscot (1) has a wingspan of 30—35 mm. There are two generations a year, which are on the wing from May till July, and from August till September. The caterpillars hibernate. They feed on various grasses.

The Scarce Wormwood has a wingspan of 37—42 mm. The wings are narrow and coloured grey. The one generation flies in June and July. The caterpillar (2) feeds in August and September on Mugwort and other species of wormwood. The pupa (3) hibernates.

146

The Mullein (4) has a wingspan of 45—50 mm. There is one generation a year, on the wing in April and May. The colourful caterpillar (5) feeds in June on the leaves and flowers of large-flowered mulleins and other mulleins such as *Verbascum lychnitis* and *V. nigrum*. It pupates in a sturdy, earthen chamber in the ground where it remains until the following spring or often even for several years.

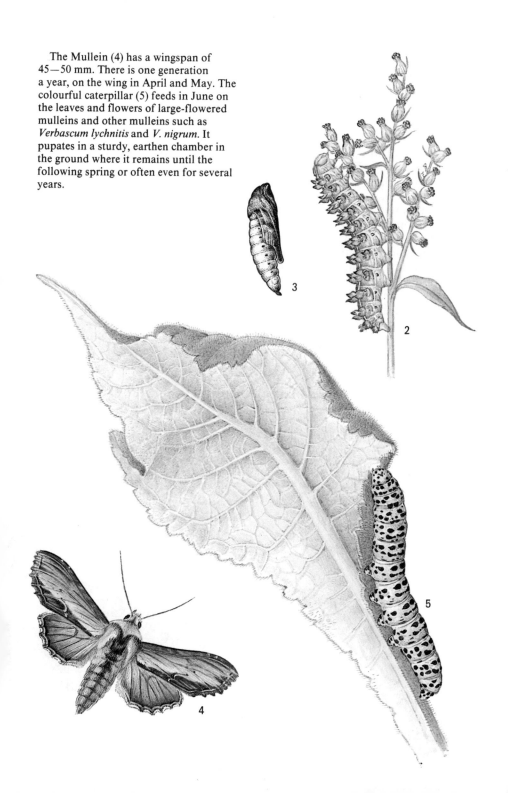

Alder Moth
Acronicta alni L.

Moths of the genus *Acronicta* s. l., particularly their caterpillars, form a distinctive group. Whereas the imagos are mostly sombrely coloured and those of various species greatly resemble each other, the hairy caterpillars are very colourful or have characteristic outgrowths on the body. The Alder is one of the most distinctively coloured moths of them all. It inhabits damp, broad-leaved forests. Though not found in the extreme southern regions of Europe, in the east its range extends to the Amur. It is generally found in lowland districts, but is occasionally present in mountains up to 1500 m. It has always been considered a fairly rare species, but in the 1980s it occurred in greater abundance in central Europe than it had for a number of years.

The Knot Grass (*A. rumicis* L.) is found in the warmer parts of the whole Palaearctic region, particularly in forestless country. It is a common moth of fields and waste places and is sometimes even a pest in gardens. The colourful caterpillars may commonly be seen in late summer in fields of Lucerne as well as other places.

The Grey Dagger (*A. psi* L.) is a moth of the steppes and is more common than two other very similar species (*A. cuspis* Hb., *A. tridens* Den. et Schiff.). These three are difficult to tell apart as imagos but readily identified as caterpillars.

A. menyanthidis View. inhabits marshes and moors and has a typical, black caterpillar.

The Alder Moth (1) has a wingspan of 33—38 mm. The one generation flies in May and June. The caterpillars (2) feed on willow, Alder, hazel etc.

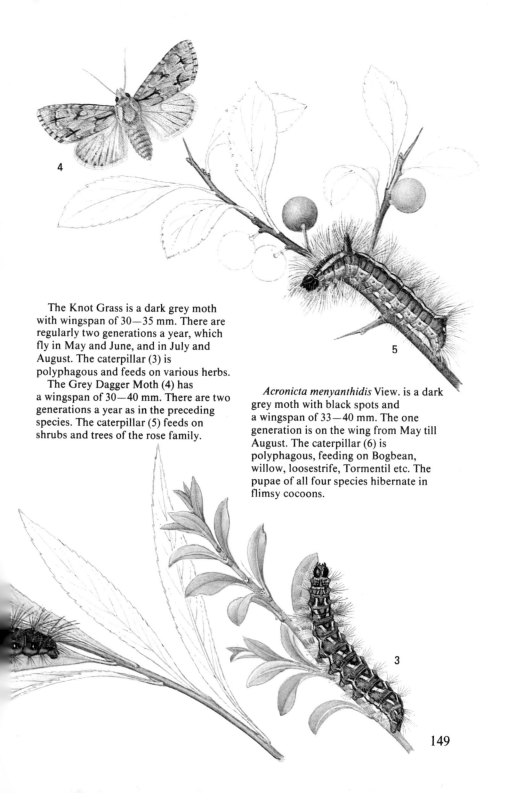

The Knot Grass is a dark grey moth with wingspan of 30—35 mm. There are regularly two generations a year, which fly in May and June, and in July and August. The caterpillar (3) is polyphagous and feeds on various herbs.

The Grey Dagger Moth (4) has a wingspan of 30—40 mm. There are two generations a year as in the preceding species. The caterpillar (5) feeds on shrubs and trees of the rose family.

Acronicta menyanthidis View. is a dark grey moth with black spots and a wingspan of 33—40 mm. The one generation is on the wing from May till August. The caterpillar (6) is polyphagous, feeding on Bogbean, willow, loosestrife, Tormentil etc. The pupae of all four species hibernate in flimsy cocoons.

149

Copper Underwing
Amphipyra pyramidea L.

Noctuidae

The subfamily Amphipyrinae includes many strikingly coloured and relatively large moths and several very large genera such as *Apamea* O. and *Caradrina* O., which have a great wealth of species. There is also the genus *Amphipyra* O., represented in Europe by nine species, of which the following two are the most common.

The Copper Underwing is commonly found in broad-leaved forests throughout Europe and Asia to Japan. Apart from forests it occurs only in places with groups of trees and shrubs, parkland and orchards. This moth does not exhibit much variation in coloration. Recently, however, a form with slightly blurred markings attracted the attention of authorities. On more detailed investigation it was discovered to be a hitherto unknown, separate species, named *A. berbera* Rungs (Svensson's Copper Underwing). So far, little is known about its distribution, but it appears to have an inclination for riparian forests and in many biotopes is more abundant than the well-known Copper Underwing.

The Mouse (*Amphipyra tragopogonis* Cl.) also is a common moth. It is widely distributed in forests as well as open countryside in the whole of Europe and Asia, but it usually escapes notice because of its inconspicuous coloration. This moth is markedly photophobic (avoids light). During the day it hides under the bark of trees, in rock crevices, beneath stones and in other similar places, and when it is uncovered it quickly tries to find another dark place. Frequently it hides also in cracks in various conveyances thereby making its way even to far distant places.

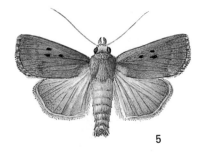

5

The Copper Underwing (1) has a wingspan of 40—52 mm. The male and female have the same colouring. The one generation a year is on the wing from July till October. The egg hibernates and the caterpillar (2) develops in spring and feeds on Common Maple, oak, birch and other trees. The pupa is a gleaming, dark brown. The copulatory organs of the male (3) serve as a means of distinguishing this moth from the similar *A. berbera* (4).

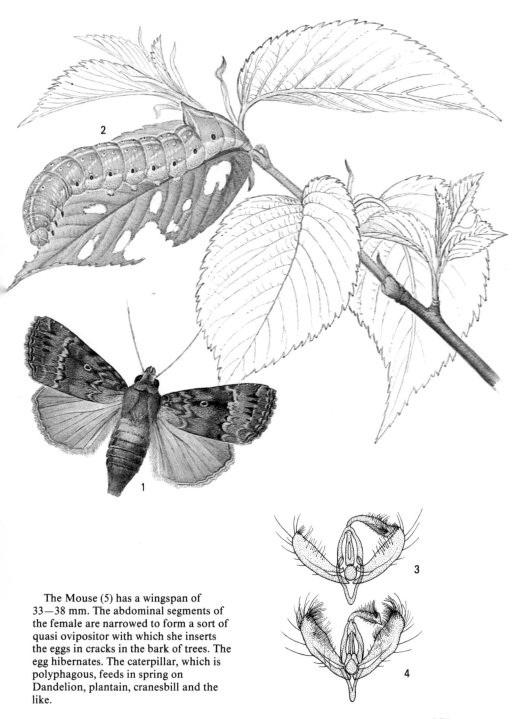

The Mouse (5) has a wingspan of
33—38 mm. The abdominal segments of
the female are narrowed to form a sort of
quasi ovipositor with which she inserts
the eggs in cracks in the bark of trees. The
egg hibernates. The caterpillar, which is
polyphagous, feeds in spring on
Dandelion, plantain, cranesbill and the
like.

Burnished Brass Moth
Diachrysia chrysitis L.

Noctuidae

The subfamily Plusiinae numbers some 40 species in Europe. These are very striking, characteristic moths. The caterpillars of some species compared with others, have two pairs of legs less, pupate in cocoons, and the pupae have the sheath of the proboscis prolonged.

The Burnished Brass Moth is very ornamental. Most of its wing surface is covered with metallic green patches. It is distributed throughout the whole Palaearctic, except the polar regions. It occurs chiefly in lowland districts where it flies about among shrubs, in forest margins and in damp valleys. It is also found in waste places around human habitations.

The Silver Y Moth (*Autographa gamma* L.) derives its name from the gleaming markings on the forewings, which resemble the Greek letter 'gamma'. It is one of the well-known migrant species that during the growing season inhabit even places where they cannot overwinter. For example, it may be found in the far north or in high mountains. It is distributed throughout the Palaearctic but winters only in temperate regions with a warm climate. Migrations cause a mix of populations from distant regions. Every year in central Europe, for example, overwintering populations mix with others arriving from subtropical regions. The Silver Y Moth sometimes causes great damage to farm crops when it overmultiplies.

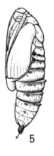

The Burnished Brass Moth (1) has a wingspan of 28—35 mm. The metallic patches on the wings sometimes join to form a horseshoe mark (2 — f. *juncta*). There are generally two generations a year, on the wing in May and June and then in July till September. The caterpillar overwinters when it is half-grown. It is polyphagous, with a special liking for deadnettle, Stinging Nettle, *Ballota* and plantain, and it pupates in a white cocoon located among plants.

152

1

2

3

4

The Silver Y Moth (3) has a wingspan of 35—40 mm. There are one to three generations a year, depending on the elevation, climate and geographic location. In central Europe the moths are on the wing from May till November; migrants from the south sometimes appear as early as April. The caterpillar (4) hibernates when half-grown. The pupa (5) is enclosed in a white cocoon among leaves or on the ground.

Clifden Nonpareil
Catocala fraxini L.

Noctuidae

Moths of the genus *Catocala* Schr. are some of the largest and without a doubt the most handsome of moths. The hind wings of the more than 25 European species are variously coloured: blue, red and yellow. The sombre forewings, however, cover and conceal this beauty so that when the moth is resting on the trunk of a tree it escapes the notice of birds. The wings are not colourful simply for beauty's sake. When danger threatens they are suddenly unmasked to startle the enemy and give the moth a chance to escape by rapid zig-zag flight. Moths of the genus *Catocala* are generally extremely wary, and it is difficult to get near them when they are resting during the day.

The Clifden Nonpareil flies in riparian and other damp broad-leaved forests in stream-filled and river valleys. Except for the dry southern regions it is distributed throughout the Palaearctic and in North America. The markings as well as the coloration of the adult moth are extremely variable. Some forms have pale greyish white forewings, whereas others have very dark wings with indistinct markings. The blue colouring ranges from bluish white to dark violet-blue.

The species *Ephesia fulminea* Sc. is a thermophilous moth of forest-steppes and steppes. It is found in suitable biotopes from Europe through all of Asia to Japan. It was formerly a relatively common moth but has disappeared in many localities, and in others is much less abundant than before due to intensive cultivation of the country-side, the clearing of shrubs and the use of pesticides.

The Clifden Nonpareil (1) has a wingspan of 75—95 mm. There is one generation a year, which is on the wing from June till October. The eggs (2) hibernate and in spring the caterpillars (3) emerge and feed on the leaves of various broad-leaved trees such as poplar, willow, ash and oak. They reach full maturity in June and July after which they pupate among leaves that are spun together. The pupa (4) is black dusted with blue. The adult moth emerges after two to three weeks.

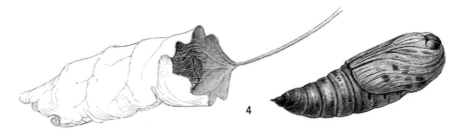

4

Ephesia fulminea Sc. (5) has a wingspan
of 45—52 mm. There is one generation
a year, on the wing from June till August.
It overwinters in the egg stage. The
caterpillar feeds in spring on Blackthorn
and wild plum, occasionally also on
Common Hawthorn. It pupates as early
as May among leaves spun together.

5

1

2

3

Red Underwing
Catocala nupta L.

Noctuidae

Of the red-coloured moths of the genus *Catocala* Schr. this one is the most abundant. It inhabits broad-leaved forests and is distributed throughout Europe as far as eastern Asia, with the exception of the driest regions in the south and those beyond the Arctic Circle. It is found mostly in forests beside streams as well as calm waters but also in rather damp mixed forests at altitudes of up to 1000 m. It also finds urban parks to its liking and thus may be often seen in large cities with marked atmospheric pollution. Like most members of this genus the adult moth has a long life span. The eggs, which mature in succession, are laid singly or in small clusters in cracks in the bark of tree trunks. For this purpose the females have a greatly narrowed abdomen and are able to deposit eggs even in deep crevices. The Red Underwing may be easily lured in the evening to bait spread on the trunks of trees. In the light of a torch lamp it is then possible to observe how the moth sucks juice with its long proboscis. Among the red-coloured moths there may very occasionally be specimens with yellow hind wings (f. *flava*).

The Dark Crimson Underwing (*Catocala sponsa* L.) has the hind wings coloured dark crimson and the markings on the forewings are more prominent than in other similar species. A thermophilic moth, it is distributed in northern Africa, Asia Minor and the temperate regions of Europe to the Urals. It is a species that is on the wing earlier than are other species of *Catocala*.

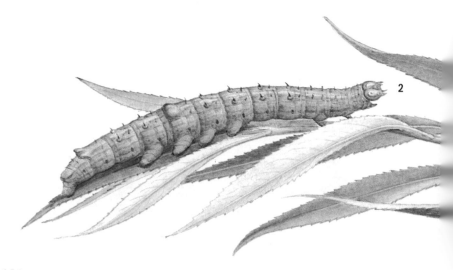

2

The Red Underwing (1) has a wingspan of 65—75 mm. The colouring of the male and the female is the same. There is one generation a year with the moths on the wing from the end of July till October. The caterpillar (2) feeds in spring on poplars and willows. The pupa (3) may be found among spun-up leaves from June till August for the development of the caterpillars (even from the same batch of eggs) is very unequal. The winter is passed in the egg stage.

The Dark Crimson Underwing (4) has a wingspan of 60—70 mm. The moths of the single generation are on the wing from the end of June until September. The eggs hibernate. The brown-grey, striped caterpillar has outgrowths on the fifth and sixth abdominal segments. It feeds in May and June on oaks.

157

Puss Moth
Cerura vinula L.

Notodontidae

The family of Prominents (Notodontidae) includes some 2000 species. Most are native to South America; only about 40 are indigenous to Europe. In this family it is the caterpillars that are of particular interest. Frequently they have outgrowths on the body or have the last pair of legs modified into fork-like appendages. The caterpillar of the illustrated Puss Moth is a typical example. When irritated it adopts a defensive posture, pulling its head inside the first thoracic segment and projecting red flagella from the fork-like appendage at the end of the abdomen. The Puss is distributed in the broad-leaved forest zone throughout the Palaearctic region. In mountains it occurs at altitudes up to 2500 m. It inhabits damp forests in stream and river valleys. The adult moth is rarely encountered in the wild, but the bizarre and brightly coloured caterpillars are often found on willows and Aspens.

The Lobster Moth (*Stauropus fagi* L.) is found in the warmer broad-leaved forests of Europe and Asia; very occasionally it may be encountered in Great Britain and Ireland and in mountains as high up as 1500 m. In southern Asia it even overmultiplies on occasion, occurring in vast numbers that cause damage in broad-leaved forests. The adult moth though large is sombrely coloured. It is often attracted to light, and once it alights nothing will disturb it; it may even be taken up in the hand. The remarkable caterpillar has extremely long front legs and in a defensive posture appears somewhat like a large spider.

3

The Puss Moth (1) has a wingspan of 45—70 mm. The male differs from the female in size and by having pectinate antennae. The moths of the one generation are on the wing from April till July, depending on the altitude. The caterpillar (2) feeds from June till September on willows and poplars. It pupates in a cocoon hardened with wood shavings and attached to a branch, where

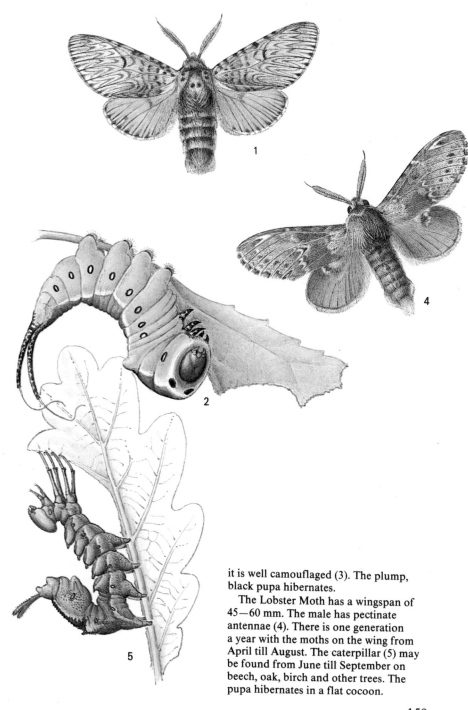

1

4

2

5

it is well camouflaged (3). The plump, black pupa hibernates.

The Lobster Moth has a wingspan of 45—60 mm. The male has pectinate antennae (4). There is one generation a year with the moths on the wing from April till August. The caterpillar (5) may be found from June till September on beech, oak, birch and other trees. The pupa hibernates in a flat cocoon.

Pebble Prominent
Eligmodonta ziczac L.

The Pebble Prominent is distributed throughout Europe and Asia as far as the Far East. It is found in lowland districts as well as in mountains up to altitudes of 2500 m, in short, wherever the food plants of the caterpillars, i.e. willows and poplars, grow. The places where it is truly at home, however, are flood plain forests, the damp margins of mixed forests, muddy forest rides, clearings, stream and river valleys. The adult moth is rarely seen, unless one decides to go hunting at night with a light and a sheet. Practically always several specimens will be attracted to the light, will fly about a while and then alight on the sheet, after which nothing will disturb them. However, an adult moth is more easily obtained from the caterpillar, which is a very strange creature compared to most other species. When resting, the rear end of the caterpillar's abdomen is raised and there are two large outgrowths or 'humps' on the forward segments. The thorax is greatly narrowed and the head large. The caterpillar is variously coloured and may be grey, brown, blue, green or violet. It appears to be very conspicuous but in reality it faithfully mimics the twisted leaves and galls on the leaves of its food plants.

Similar, with several 'humps' on the back, is the caterpillar of the Iron Prominent (*Notodonta dromedarius* L.), distributed in the forest zone of Europe and Asia. It is found in lowland as well as mountain districts in mixed woods and on the margins of moors. It is common also in city parks and places with larger groups of trees.

4

The Pebble Prominent (1) has a wingspan of 40—45 mm. The male has pectinate (comb-like) antennae, whereas those of the female are setaceous (bristle-like). There are one or two generations a year, depending on the climatic conditions and height of the locality. If there is one generation the moths are on the wing in June and July; if there are two, they fly from April till August. The caterpillar (2) feeds in summer or autumn on Goat Willow and other willows, occasionally

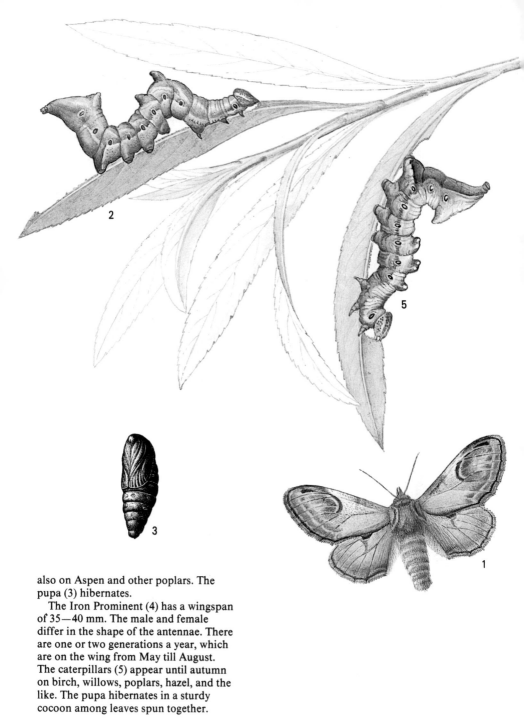

also on Aspen and other poplars. The pupa (3) hibernates.

The Iron Prominent (4) has a wingspan of 35—40 mm. The male and female differ in the shape of the antennae. There are one or two generations a year, which are on the wing from May till August. The caterpillars (5) appear until autumn on birch, willows, poplars, hazel, and the like. The pupa hibernates in a sturdy cocoon among leaves spun together.

Buff-tip
Phalera bucephala L.

Only a few species of notodontids have hairy caterpillars — a striking contrast to the smooth, bizzare caterpillars of other members of this family. The Buff-tip is a relatively abundant moth coloured a silvery hue with large, yellow, circular patches at the outer edge of the wings. The hairy caterpillars live gregariously at first, several of them resting one beside the other with hind ends raised. Only in the last stage of their development, when the supply of food in the small space becomes insufficient, do they spread out on the treetops. Even so, they strip all the leaves from the branches. This species is distributed in Europe and Asia to the Far East. It inhabits broad-leaved and mixed forests and is commonly found also in large cities. The imago lives concealed from view but is attracted to light.

Of the several species of the genus *Pygaera* O., which is usually divided into two separate genera (*Pygaera* O. and *Clostera* Sam.), the most common is the Chocolate-tip (*Pygaera curtula* L.). It is distributed in the forest zone throughout the Palaearctic region. Its favourite haunts are damp places near water. The colourful, hairy caterpillar lives in spun-up leaves. So does the caterpillar of the Small Chocolate-tip (*Pygaera pigra* Hfn.). This species is more cold-loving and is abundant chiefly in mountain districts up to altitudes of 2500 m, on moors and in damp meadows.

3

5

162

The Buff-tip (1) has a wingspan of 42—55 mm. The male is smaller than the female. The moths of the single generation are on the wing from May till July. The caterpillar (2) develops from July till September, when it burrows into the ground and changes into a black pupa (3) inside an earthen cell. The pupa hibernates, frequently even twice, before the adult moth emerges. The caterpillar may be found on lime, oak, willow, hazel, etc.

The Chocolate-tip (4) has a wingspan of 27—35 mm. The male differs from the female by having pectinate antennae. There are two generations a year with the moths on the wing from May till August. The caterpillar lives on poplars and willows. The pupa hibernates.

The Small Chocolate-tip (5) has a wingspan of 22—27 mm. The sexual dimorphism, development, and number of generations are the same as for the Chocolate-tip. The caterpillar lives in spun-up leaves at the tops of young willows and poplars, mainly Goat Willow and Aspen.

163

Eyed Hawkmoth
Smerinthus ocellata L.

Sphingidae

Hawkmoths are some of the largest moths in the world. They include some 1000 species, most of them native to the tropics. Only about 20 species live in Europe. Among them is a group of moths with rudimentary mouthparts and therefore unable to feed. These have shaggy bodies and the outer margins of the wings have pronounced or less pronounced indentations. When at rest they hold the wings horizontal, not clasped in a roof-like manner over the body like in other hawkmoths. The caterpillars are coarsely grainy, both the head and the entire body. Of this group four species live in Europe. The four were formerly classed in the genus *Smerinthus* Latr., but only the well-known Eyed Hawkmoth has remained there; the rest were transferred to other newly-formed genera. The Eyed Hawkmoth is distributed in Europe and western Asia, where it inhabits riparian forests and shoreline vegetation. It is quite abundant throughout its range, occurring from lowlands to as high up in the mountains as approximately 2000 m. It may also be seen in city parks, orchards and vineyards. It is active at night.

Another of this group that is also abundant is the Poplar Hawkmoth (*Laothoe populi* L.), distributed throughout all of Europe and Asia to the Altai. It is found chiefly in lowland districts but may also be present in mountains up to 1600 m in localities similar to those of the preceding species. Its coloration is relatively variable. It flies only at night and is attracted to light usually after midnight.

3

The Eyed Hawkmoth (1) has a wingspan of 70—80 mm. There is one generation a year with the moths on the wing from May till August. The caterpillar (2) lives from June till September on willows, poplars, apple and other trees. One of the features that distinguishes it from the similar caterpillars of other species is the blue 'horn' on the hind end. It pupates in the ground. The pupa (3), blackish brown to black with a slight sheen, hibernates.

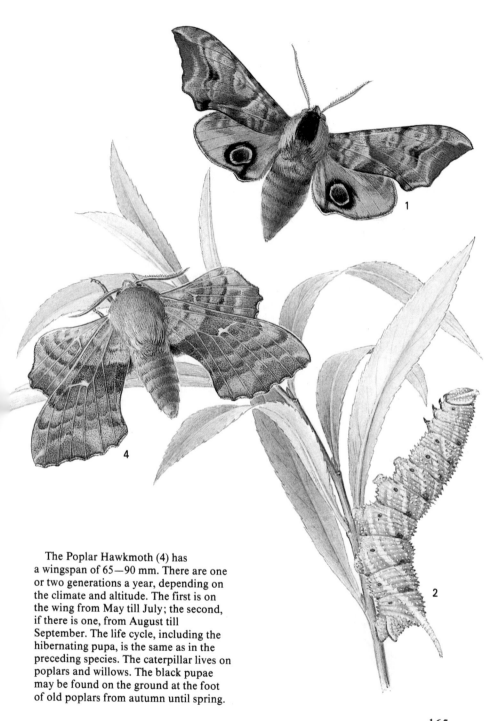

The Poplar Hawkmoth (4) has a wingspan of 65—90 mm. There are one or two generations a year, depending on the climate and altitude. The first is on the wing from May till July; the second, if there is one, from August till September. The life cycle, including the hibernating pupa, is the same as in the preceding species. The caterpillar lives on poplars and willows. The black pupae may be found on the ground at the foot of old poplars from autumn until spring.

Death's-head Hawkmoth
Acherontia atropos L.

Hawkmoths are noted for their excellent, sustained flight. They have firm, narrow wings, strong muscles and an aerodynamically shaped body. For them, covering distances of thousands of kilometres is no problem. One of the most important migrants is the Death's-head Hawkmoth, so named in many different languages because the markings on the thorax resemble a human skull. The permanent home of this species is tropical Africa and southwestern Asia. From there, however, it makes long flights every year in various directions, appearing as a visitor even in Europe. There the female lays her eggs, from which the caterpillars emerge, are fully grown by the end of summer and then pupate. The pupae usually perish in the ground, for the moths require a much higher temperature to hatch than is usually provided by the autumn weather in central Europe. Very occasionally the pupa hibernates and the moth emerges in spring. The large pupae of the Death's-head Hawkmoth may occasionally be found when ploughing up potatoes, and adult moths may be obtained from these by keeping them in a warm place.

  Central and northern Europe are also visited regularly by another large migrant species, the Convolvulus Hawkmoth (*Agrius convolvuli* L.), though it does not live there permanently. The adult moths have an unusually long proboscis (up to 10 cm), which enables them to suck nectar even from deep, trumpet-shaped flowers such as those of tobacco and petunias. During the day they may be found resting on tree trunks, fences, walls and the like.

3

The Death's-head Hawkmoth (1) has a wingspan of 80—120 mm. In June and July moths from the tropics arrive in Europe, where one generation of caterpillars (2) develops during the summer. The pupa (3), measuring 5—7 cm long, rests deep in the soil (15—40 cm below the surface) in an earthen cell. Should moths emerge from the pupae, which happens only very occasionally, they are on the wing from September till November. The caterpillars feed on various plants of the nightshade family, e. g. Black Nightshade,

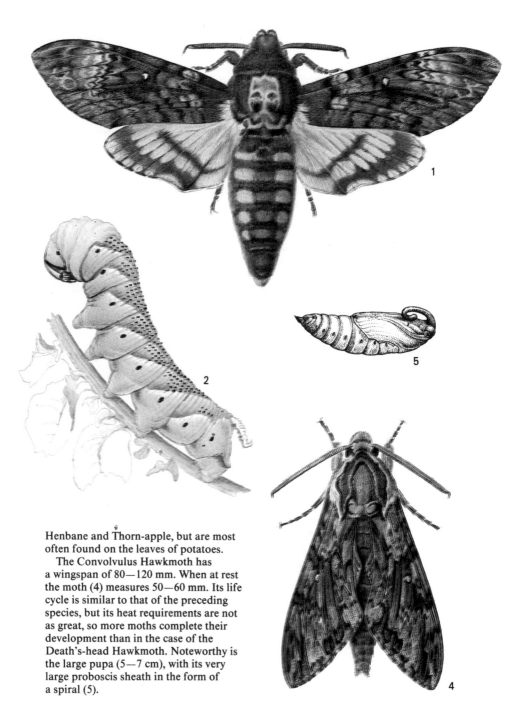

Henbane and Thorn-apple, but are most
often found on the leaves of potatoes.

The Convolvulus Hawkmoth has
a wingspan of 80—120 mm. When at rest
the moth (4) measures 50—60 mm. Its life
cycle is similar to that of the preceding
species, but its heat requirements are not
as great, so more moths complete their
development than in the case of the
Death's-head Hawkmoth. Noteworthy is
the large pupa (5—7 cm), with its very
large proboscis sheath in the form of
a spiral (5).

167

Privet Hawkmoth

Sphingidae

Sphinx ligustri L.

This hawkmoth is distributed throughout the Palaearctic region from northern Africa and Europe to Japan. It is absent only from the cold, northern regions; though caught there a number of times, the captured specimens were always individuals that had wandered there and whose offspring could not survive the cruel winter. In central Europe the Privet Hawkmoth is an indigenous species that occurs in relative abundance. On warm evenings it begins flying as soon as dusk falls, sucking nectar from the trumpet-shaped flowers of various plants and shrubs. Its movements within its range of distribution appear to be rather complex. Local populations are apparently augmented throughout the summer by arrivals from the south. Only thus is it possible to explain the occurrence of the moths in central Europe in August, when it is still too early for a possible second local generation and too late for the first.

The Pine Hawkmoth (*Hyloicus pinastri* L.) is a common species of coniferous forests, particularly rather dry ones. It is distributed throughout all of Europe except for the south, its range in the east extending beyond the Urals to Lake Baikal. It is an excellent flier and apparently roams the countryside even within the boundaries of the region it inhabits, for it has been observed far from coniferous forests. It is considered a pest by foresters. During the twentieth century melanistic form (f. *unicolor*) began to appear in industrial regions.

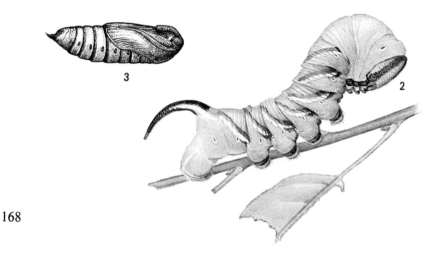

3

2

168

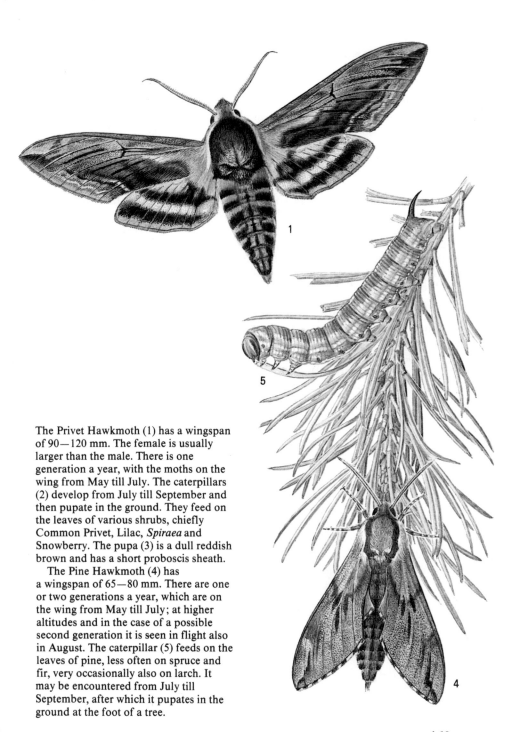

The Privet Hawkmoth (1) has a wingspan of 90—120 mm. The female is usually larger than the male. There is one generation a year, with the moths on the wing from May till July. The caterpillars (2) develop from July till September and then pupate in the ground. They feed on the leaves of various shrubs, chiefly Common Privet, Lilac, *Spiraea* and Snowberry. The pupa (3) is a dull reddish brown and has a short proboscis sheath.

The Pine Hawkmoth (4) has a wingspan of 65—80 mm. There are one or two generations a year, which are on the wing from May till July; at higher altitudes and in the case of a possible second generation it is seen in flight also in August. The caterpillar (5) feeds on the leaves of pine, less often on spruce and fir, very occasionally also on larch. It may be encountered from July till September, after which it pupates in the ground at the foot of a tree.

Spurge Hawkmoth
Hyles euphorbiae L.

Sphingidae

The Spurge Hawkmoth inhabits central and southern Europe and western Asia to northern India. In England it is considered a rare guest. In central Europe it has declined markedly in number. As late as the 1940s the caterpillars could be found everywhere on spurge in summer. Nowadays this moth is a rare species and in many areas has become extinct. In farm country the use of pesticides was responsible for this, but it seems that the causes are more profound, perhaps even global. The Spurge Hawkmoth prefers steppe localities and sand dunes, but it is also found in farming country in hedgerows, and on pasture and fallow land. It is interesting to observe the reactions of these moths to light. Although they are active from sunset throughout the night, they are not attracted to lights until around midnight, sometimes in great numbers. The coloration of the moths is quite variable. One often sees forms with the forewings flushed pink or with brown-speckled wings.

The similar Bedstraw Hawkmoth (*Hyles gali* Rott.) is distributed from Europe through Asia to North America. It is absent only from the polar regions. In mountains it occurs at altitudes up to 2000 m. In comparison with the Spurge Hawk it is considered a rare species, but during some periods there is a shift and then it occurs in greater numbers for several years in succession.

The Spurge Hawkmoth (1) has a wingspan of 55—75 mm. The female is usually larger than the male. In cooler regions there is one generation a year, in warmer climates two, and they are on the wing from May till August. The caterpillars (2) complete their development at the beginning of August, and those of the second generation may still be found in September and early October. The pupa (3) hibernates in

a cocoon of plant remains on the ground or in an earthen cell that is not very sturdy just beneath the surface.

The Bedstraw Hawkmoth (4) has a wingspan of 60—80 mm. It, too, has one or two generations between May and September. The caterpillar is similar to that of the Spurge Hawkmoth but is less colourful and darker. The pupa is very similar as well.

Elephant Hawkmoth
Deilephila elpenor L.

Sphingidae

This species is a common European hawkmoth, absent only from the north. In the east its range extends to Japan. It is most abundant at medium and submontane levels but may be found also in mountains up to 1500 m. Its favourite haunts are wooded mountain valleys, forest clearings with tall herbaceous growth and, at lower altitudes, the shoreline vegetation by streams, rivers and ponds. Although the caterpillars have been found on many plants, including fruit trees and grape vines, the Elephant Hawkmoth nevertheless seems to be partial to two particular plants: Rosebay Willow herb or Fireweed in forests and mountain valleys and *Epilobium hirsutum* in forests and mountain valleys. Interesting characteristics of the caterpillar are the shape of the body (it narrows suddenly and markedly towards the head) and the thoracic segment markings, which resemble eyes and are intended to frighten off possible attackers.

The Small Elephant Hawkmoth (*Deilephila porcellus* L.) is a sort of miniature Elephant Hawkmoth. The caterpillars also are quite similar. This moth, widely distributed in Europe and Asia to the Altai, inhabits grassy areas that are rich in flowering herbs and the edges of forests in steppe and forest-steppe regions. It is also plentiful in cities wherever there is plenty of greenery. It is rarely seen during the day, but at night it often comes to light. The coloration is very variable, ranging from pink to dark carmine red plus various shades of green on the forewings; the hind wings are often nearly black.

4

The Elephant Hawkmoth (1) has a wingspan of 45—60 mm. There is one generation a year. The period when the moths are on the wing depends on the altitude but is between May and July or even later. The caterpillar is polyphagous and lives from May till September. There are two forms: a brown form (2) and a green form (3). The pupa (4) hibernates. It has a large cremaster.

The Small Elephant Hawkmoth (5) has a wingspan of 40—45 mm and is one of the smallest hawkmoths. There is one generation a year, in warmer years also a partial second generation. The moths of the first generation fly from May till the beginning of July; those of the second may be encountered in August. The caterpillar lives in summer on bedstraw, willowherb and other plants. The long, slender pupa hibernates in the ground.

Hummingbird Hawkmoth
Macroglossum stellatarum L.

Sphingidae

The Hummingbird Hawkmoth inhabits the warmer parts of the Palae-arctic region and recently was found also in North America. It is such a pronounced migrant, however, that it is difficult to determine the boundaries of its permanent distribution. In years of massive migration it may suddenly appear even in polar regions or in mountains by the edges of glaciers as high up as 3000 m, where the females lay eggs and the resulting progeny may survive for a number of years. Afterwards the species retreats south. In central Europe on several occasions hibernating pupae have been known to survive the winter successfully, but then it has seemed as though the species has disappeared again. This small hawkmoth is on the wing during the day and is probably one of the fastest fliers in the insect world. Whirring its wings it remains hovering in the same spot while sucking nectar from flowers with its long proboscis. In the sunlight the shiny, green, bulging eyes are striking. When the moth has sucked all the nectar from one flower, it moves with lightning speed a few metres further on to another. It likes to rest on sun-warmed ground and stones. On hot days it is extremely wary and flies off in a flash. It is interesting to note the hairs and scales expanding the supporting surface of the abdomen; these apparently serve as stabilizers during rapid flight.

Another small hawkmoth — the Willowherb Hawkmoth (*Proserpinus proserpina* Pall.), is an oriental, thermophilous species whose range extends through Asia to the warmer parts of Europe. It is found in sandy places and in lowland districts by streams and rivers. It flies by night. Of late it is unfortunately joining the ranks of endangered species.

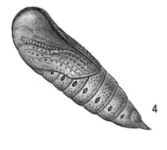

4

The Hummingbird Hawkmoth (1) has a wingspan of 40—50 mm. There are two generations a year. The first generally arrives from the south between April and June; the second is on the wing from August till October. The green or brown caterpillars (2, 3) live on bedstraw in July and August or in the autumn. The pupa (4) hibernates. Some years the species

occurs in abundance, but other years it is rare, depending on migrations.

The Willowherb Hawkmoth (5) has a wingspan of 37—42 mm. Moths of the single generation are on the wing in May and June. The caterpillar lives in July and August on Evening Primrose and *Epilobium hirsutum*. The pupa hibernates.

Greater or **Viennese Emperor**
Saturnia pyri Den et Schiff.

Saturniidae

The Greater or Viennese Emperor is the largest European Moth, widespread in the Mediterranean region, both in its European and African parts. Central Europe is the northern limit of its European range, which extends eastwards through Asia Minor, the Caucasus and Transcaucasia to the Middle East. Everything about this moth is large. The eggs measure nearly 3 mm, the caterpillars are about 10 cm long, the cocoon is big, and the pupa is stout. The adult moth does not feed, surviving instead on the fat reserves accumulated by the caterpillar.

The Greater Emperor may be found in spring, sitting with slightly open wings on tree trunks close by the large, brownish grey cocoon. At other times at night it may be found resting on a wall on which light shines from a nearby street lamp. Also at night the moths may be seen whirling around street lamps and casting large shadows on the ground. Due to its size it is more like a bat than an insect.

Originally this moth inhabited forest-steppe areas, but long ago it became adapted to life in fruit tree nurseries and orchards in so-called cultivated steppe. Here it fell victim to the inexorable effects of civilization, and in the last few decades its numbers have been so reduced because of the effects of chemicals that many countries are justifiably considering the need for its protection. This lovely product of nature can survive only in protected forest-steppe ecosystems and in cultivated country where plants are not treated with chemicals.

4

3

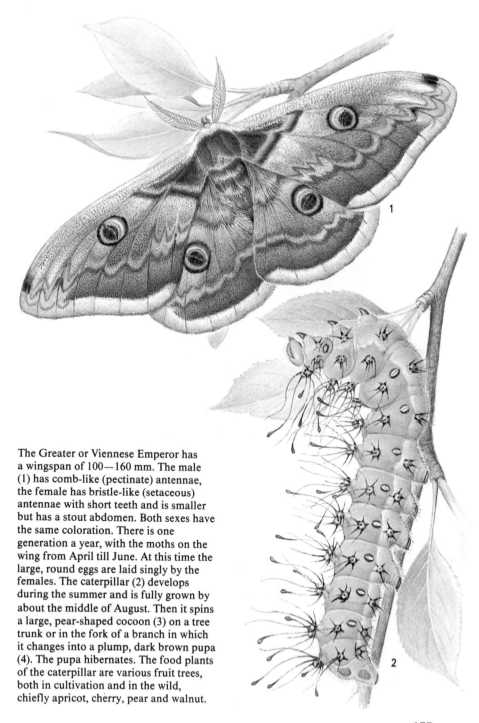

The Greater or Viennese Emperor has a wingspan of 100—160 mm. The male (1) has comb-like (pectinate) antennae, the female has bristle-like (setaceous) antennae with short teeth and is smaller but has a stout abdomen. Both sexes have the same coloration. There is one generation a year, with the moths on the wing from April till June. At this time the large, round eggs are laid singly by the females. The caterpillar (2) develops during the summer and is fully grown by about the middle of August. Then it spins a large, pear-shaped cocoon (3) on a tree trunk or in the fork of a branch in which it changes into a plump, dark brown pupa (4). The pupa hibernates. The food plants of the caterpillar are various fruit trees, both in cultivation and in the wild, chiefly apricot, cherry, pear and walnut.

177

Emperor Moth
Saturnia pavonia L.   Saturniidae

The Emperor Moth, widespread throughout all Europe and Asia to the Far East, inhabits not only forest-steppe areas but also rocky steppes and the zone of broad-leaved and mixed forests. In mountains it may be found at altitudes of up to 2000 m. Its occurrence on mountain moors is that this species can withstand very rugged conditions practically like those in the tundra. The males are on the wing on sunny afternoons in spring, the females are active at night and occasionally respond to light. The caterpillars undergo a number of colour changes after hatching. At first they are completely black, but after the first moult they have orange spots, and these become larger in succeeding instars (growth stages). Not until they are fully grown do the caterpillars acquire their typical, black and green coloration, which, however, is extremely variable: in some individuals the green is very limited giving way to extensive areas of black, whereas in others the green prevails and the black markings are limited to small patches. Mountain populations are usually dark and lowland populations light-coloured.

The Tau Emperor (*Aglia tau* L.) is sometimes placed in a separate family, the Syssphingidae. It is distributed in broad-leaved forests throughout the Palaearctic region, excepting the British Isles, from lowland districts to the upper limit of beech forests, primarily at altitudes of about 300—500 m. The male flies during the morning but responds to light at night. The female flies only at night. This moth often occurs as a dark form. The form *ferenigra* is entirely black, but more common are intermediately coloured, transitional forms varying in the degree of the dark colouring.

6

3

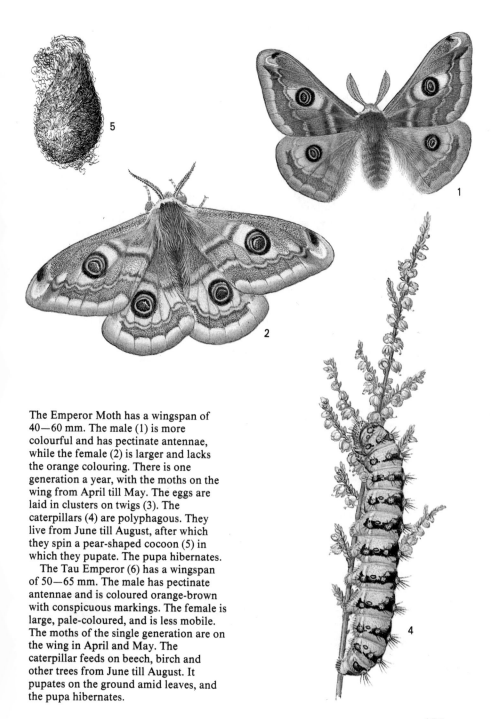

The Emperor Moth has a wingspan of 40—60 mm. The male (1) is more colourful and has pectinate antennae, while the female (2) is larger and lacks the orange colouring. There is one generation a year, with the moths on the wing from April till May. The eggs are laid in clusters on twigs (3). The caterpillars (4) are polyphagous. They live from June till August, after which they spin a pear-shaped cocoon (5) in which they pupate. The pupa hibernates.

The Tau Emperor (6) has a wingspan of 50—65 mm. The male has pectinate antennae and is coloured orange-brown with conspicuous markings. The female is large, pale-coloured, and is less mobile. The moths of the single generation are on the wing in April and May. The caterpillar feeds on beech, birch and other trees from June till August. It pupates on the ground amid leaves, and the pupa hibernates.

179

Drinker
Philudoria potatoria L.

The family of eggars is distributed principally in the tropics. It is absent from New Zealand and Oceania and is represented by a great number of species in South America. There are some 1300 species worldwide; about 20 are found in Europe. They are medium- to large-sized moths with shaggy body and broad wings usually coloured yellow-brown. The mouthparts are degenerate, and the females are markedly different from the males. The slow-crawling caterpillars are relatively large and hairy. All these characteristics apply also to the Drinker, distributed in the temperate zone throughout the Palaearctic region, from western Europe to Japan. Within this range, however, it occurs only locally in suitable, damp, grassy habitats. It frequents also the sandy substrates beside rivers and streams. The moth's coloration is very variable, and the female is paler than the male. During the past decades the Drinker has disappeared from many localities and elsewhere has become rarer than before.

The Lackey (*Malacosoma neustria* L.) is a well-known pest of fruit trees and is distributed throughout all Europe and Asia. It used to inhabit forest-steppe areas, but with the disappearance of its original biotopes it found a substitute biotope in fruit orchards. It is interesting to note that disastrous infestations do not occur several times in succession in the same place but always shift to several kilometres away every year. The coloration of the moth is variable, ranging from pale yellow to dark brown.

The Drinker (1) has a wingspan of 45—65 mm. The male has pectinate antennae. There is one generation a year. The moths fly at night from June to August. As in most members of this family the development of the caterpillars (2) is slow. They hibernate before they are fully grown and pupate in May or June in a cocoon amid vegetation. They feed on various grasses.

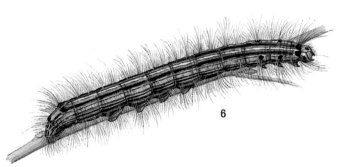

6

4

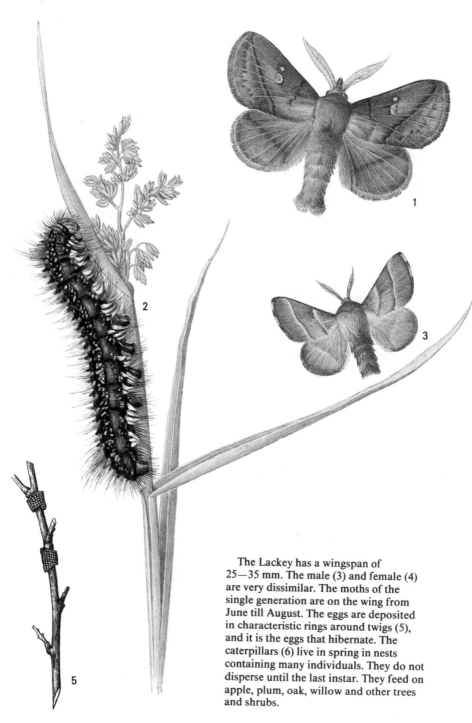

The Lackey has a wingspan of
25—35 mm. The male (3) and female (4)
are very dissimilar. The moths of the
single generation are on the wing from
June till August. The eggs are deposited
in characteristic rings around twigs (5),
and it is the eggs that hibernate. The
caterpillars (6) live in spring in nests
containing many individuals. They do not
disperse until the last instar. They feed on
apple, plum, oak, willow and other trees
and shrubs.

181

Lappet
Gastropacha quercifolia L.

Lasiocampidae

The Lappet is the largest of the European eggars to have a range extending eastwards to Japan. It occurs naturally in thin broad-leaved woods in warmer areas, particularly in forest-steppe, and has also become well adapted to agricultural areas with many fruit trees and shrubs. Formerly it was a pest, but because intensive cultivation of fruit with the use of chemicals is not conducive to its well-being it is now limited to old, neglected orchards and shrubby pastureland and has become a rather rare species. Northern Europe is the home of the dark form *alnifolia*, and in the south is found the pale form *meridionalis*. The caterpillars are large but coloured to resemble twigs, so they are difficult to locate in the wild. They spin large, grey cocoons for themselves in among the branches.

One of the commonest moths of this family is the Fox (*Macrothylacia rubi* L.). Except for the extreme north, it is to be found everywhere, primarily in lowland districts but also in mountains up to altitudes of 1500 m. The males take to the air before sunset, moving about in swift, darting flight until dusk. The females are nocturnal in habit. They often fly towards light and generally deposit eggs wherever they settle. The coloration of the caterpillar is interesting in the penultimate instar; it is black-brown with orange stripes between the individual segments.

The Lappet (1) has a wingspan of 50—90 mm. When at rest the moth (2) closes its wings so that it completely resembles a dry twisted leaf. Sexual dimorphism is evident in the size of the

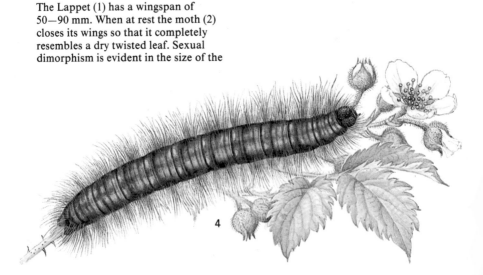

4

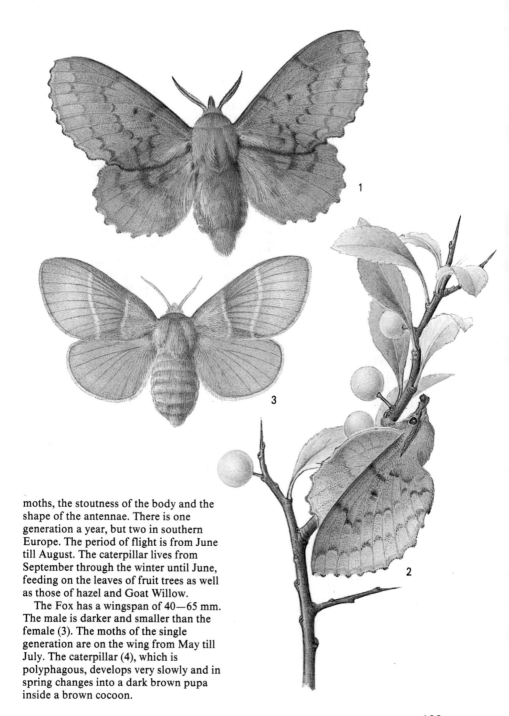

moths, the stoutness of the body and the shape of the antennae. There is one generation a year, but two in southern Europe. The period of flight is from June till August. The caterpillar lives from September through the winter until June, feeding on the leaves of fruit trees as well as those of hazel and Goat Willow.

The Fox has a wingspan of 40—65 mm. The male is darker and smaller than the female (3). The moths of the single generation are on the wing from May till July. The caterpillar (4), which is polyphagous, develops very slowly and in spring changes into a dark brown pupa inside a brown cocoon.

Oak Eggar
Lasiocampa quercus L.

Lasiocampidae

The freshly hatched male of this large eggar is a truly beautiful creature. The paler and larger female is not nearly as colourful. The females move about in cumbersome flight late in the afternoon, but will respond to light even at night. The males dart about on sunny days in wild, zig-zag flight. Catching a male in flight with a net is a masterly feat or more likely a stroke of luck. That is why most specimens in collections are ones that have been reared. The dark, hairy caterpillars, up to 8 cm long, are found quite frequently in forests. Rearing moths from the eggs is a laborious task, even though the captured female lays them very willingly. The caterpillars develop very slowly and quite a few perish during hibernation. The Oak Eggar is widely distributed in the forests of Europe and Asia, from lowland districts to high mountains, but nowhere is it particularly abundant.

The Pine-tree Lappet (*Dendrolimus pini* L.) is a common species of coniferous and mixed forests throughout the whole Palaearctic region except north Africa, southern Europe, the British Isles and Ireland. It is an occasional forest pest, with outbreaks occurring at lengthy intervals, in cycles of several decades, chiefly in rather dry pine monocultures. It is an extremely variable moth in terms of coloration. There is also a marked difference between the male and female, the male being much more colourful. There is a brightly coloured form, *montana*, which occurs in mountains, and a dark form, *obscura*, found in moors. Paler specimens (form *grisescens*) are often seen in lowland districts.

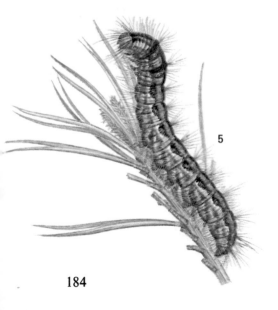

5

The Oak Eggar (1) has a wingspan of 45—75 mm. It exhibits marked sexual dimorphism. There is one generation a year, with the moths on the wing from June till August (depending on the altitude). The caterpillar (2), which is polyphagous, lives from August through the winter until May. It feeds most frequently on Bilberry, Goat Willow, heather, and oak. It pupates in an oval cocoon (3).

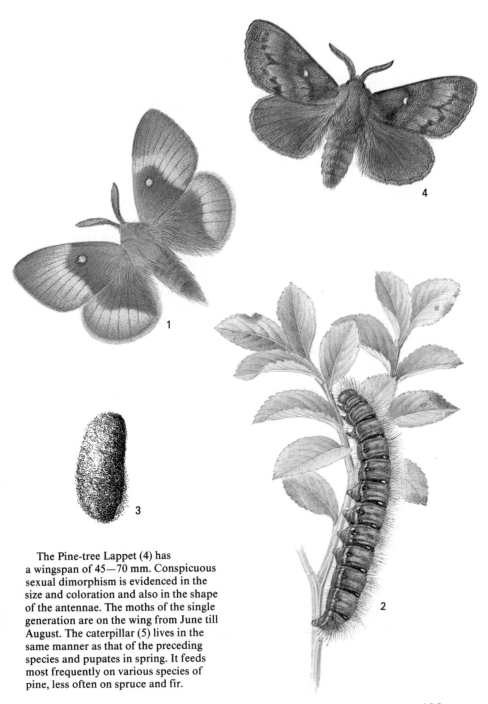

The Pine-tree Lappet (4) has a wingspan of 45—70 mm. Conspicuous sexual dimorphism is evidenced in the size and coloration and also in the shape of the antennae. The moths of the single generation are on the wing from June till August. The caterpillar (5) lives in the same manner as that of the preceding species and pupates in spring. It feeds most frequently on various species of pine, less often on spruce and fir.

185

Kentish Glory
Endromis versicolora L.

Endromidae

The Kentish Glory is one of nature's spring gems and a moth that is noteworthy in several respects. It is the only representative of a monotypic family, which means that throughout the world there is not a single related species. The Endromidae family has only one genus, *Endromis* O., with a single species, *versicolora* L. This moth has an extensive range. It is found in forests and forest-steppe areas throughout the temperate zone of the Palaearctic where various species of birch grow. In other words it occurs in all of Europe, and in Asia in the greater part of Siberia to the Far East.

The moth is on the wing in early spring (sometimes as early as March) in damp woods and groves with birches, but on moors and in mountains it does not begin to fly until May. The female flies only at night, while the male is about both at night and during the day. The males' diurnal activity is very striking, according to a certain daily rhythm. They can be seen flying about on sunny mornings between 10 and 12 o'clock in rapid, zig-zag flight. In some places they are very abundant but practically impossible to catch. The best method of obtaining specimens is by going out on a very cold morning and striking the trunks of birches, whereupon the stiff and numb moths fall to the ground. The moths are also attracted to light.

The Kentish Glory is still quite a common moth but its numbers were larger in former times. The reason for its decline is apparently the current forestry practice, perhaps also atmospheric pollution.

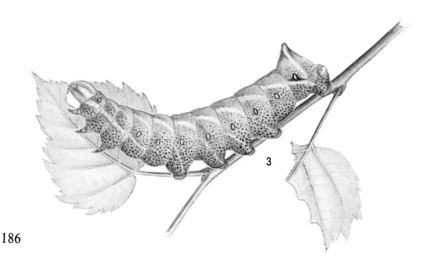

3

The Kentish Glory has a wingspan of
45—60 mm. The male (1) is colourful, has
pectinate antennae and a slender, hairy
body. The female (2) is larger and whiter,
has a stouter abdomen and the comb-like
antennae have shorter rami (branches).
There is one generation a year. The moths
are on the wing from March till May. The
caterpillar (3) lives from May till July and
feeds on the leaves of birch, hornbeam,
hazel, and very occasionally also on
alder, lime and other trees. The pupa (4)
is dark grey-brown and finely grainy. It
lies in the litter on the ground inside
a chamber made of spun-up, dry leaves
and bits of soil. The moth emerges
following hibernation, sometimes not
until a few years later.

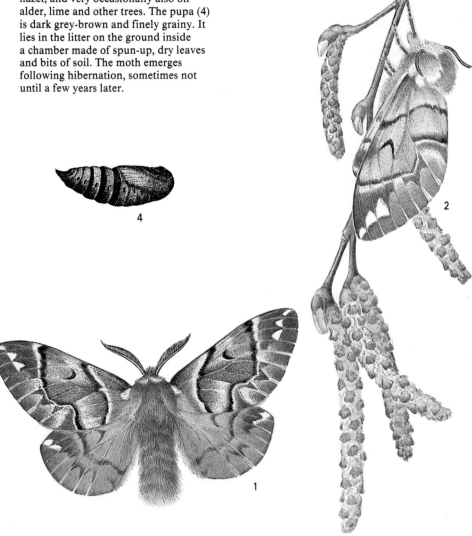

4

2

1

Peach Blossom
Thyatira batis L.

Thyatiridae

The Thyatiridae is a small family that worldwide includes some 150 species distributed in Europe, Asia and North America. Europe is the home of approximately 20 species, of which the Peach Blossom is without doubt one of the most attractive. It occurs in the temperate zone from western Europe to Japan and is a woodland species found in abundance wherever there are rather thin woods and forest clearings with wild Raspberry and Blackberry bushes. Frequently it may be encountered by streams in mountain valleys up to altitudes of 1500 m, as well as in lowland districts in damp woodland localities such as the unflooded parts of riverine forests, in shoreline thickets and the like. It flies only at night. The markings on the forewings are quite variable but always retain the basic pattern. The variability is evident only on closer examination of a number of specimens.

Another ornamental member of this family, the Buff Arches Moth (*Habrosyne pyritoides* Hfn.), has an even greater range. It occurs in relative abundance in all forests from lowland to mountain elevations. It is also found in forest-steppe and in cultivated areas in gardens and parks. The moths show little variability in coloration. In Europe the Buff Arches is the only species of this genus. The nearest place where one will find related species is the eastern part of the Palaearctic region.

3

5

The Peach Blossom (1) has a wingspan of 32—38 mm. There is no sexual dimorphism. There are two generations a year with the moths being on the wing from May till July and then again in August. In cooler climates there is only one generation, and this flies in June and July. The caterpillar (2) lives on wild Raspberry and Blackberry from July till September. It pupates among the spun-up leaves of plants or on the

ground. The pupa (3) hibernates.

The Buff Arches Moth (4) has
a wingspan of 35—40 mm. There is no
difference in the colouring of the male
and female. The moth is very shaggy (5).
There is one generation a year with the
moths on the wing from June till August.
The caterpillars are fully grown in
autumn, like those of the preceding
species. It is the pupa that hibernates.

Orange Underwing
Archiearis parthenias L.

Geometridae

The large family of geometrids numbers some 4000 species, distributed throughout the world on all continents. Approximately 800 live in
Europe. They are moths with a slender body and broad wings. The
females of many species have vestigial wings. A typical characteristic
of geometrids is the ciliated organ on the head of adult moths called
the chaetosema. Its function has not been fully explained as yet. The
caterpillars have a reduced number of legs as a consequence of which
they travel by their well-known 'looping' (inchworm) movement.

The Orange Underwing is distributed in the temperate and colder
regions of the Palaearctic. It is a forest species dependent on the presence of birch. In mountains it ascends to the upper forest limit and in
the north extends to the tundra. It is the most common of three similar European species, of which the Light Orange Underwing (*A. no-
tha* Hb.) is restricted to the Aspen and the thermophilous *A. puella*
Esp., with yellow hind wings, to other poplar species. Distinguishing
between the two orange-coloured species is quite difficult, particularly in the case of the females, which have similar antennae.

The Winter Moth (*Operophtera brumata* L.) is found in forests
throughout Eurasia and is a pest in forests and fruit orchards. The caterpillars often strip the trees bare. Though small, they occur in great
numbers. The moths are on the wing in late autumn, during the period of frost, snow and sleet. The males fly at night; during the day
they rest inconspicuously on tree trunks. The females have vestigial
wings; at night they always climb up tree trunks to the crown; by day
they hide in the grass at the foot of the tree.

5

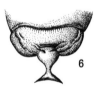

6

3

The Orange Underwing (1) has
a wingspan of 30—40 mm. There is one
generation a year with the moths on the
wing in March and April. The caterpillar
lives from April till June, feeding on
birch. It pupates on the ground and the
pupa overwinters until spring.

The male Winter Moth (2) has a wingspan of 22—28 mm. The female (3) has vestigial wings and is 8—10 mm long. The moths of the single generation are on the wing from September till December. The eggs hibernate. The caterpillars (4), which are polyphagous, hatch in spring and are fully grown in May. They can live on practically all broad-leaved trees and shrubs. They pupate in the ground. The pupa (5), with its characteristically shaped cremaster (6), rests until autumn. The drop in temperature then stimulates the hatching of the moths.

Phoenix
Eulithis prunata L.

Geometridae

The subfamily Larentiinae includes many medium-sized and small species with very richly patterned forewings. The Phoenix is one of the larger species. It has a large range of distribution in Europe, Asia and North America and is relatively abundant throughout. It occurs in forest-steppe areas and in the margins of broad-leaved forests where it flies about at night, like most geometrids.

The Garden Carpet (*Xanthorhoe fluctuata* L.) is one of the most abundant geometrid moths. Most geometrids are woodland species, but this moth is one of the exceptions. It may be encountered practically everywhere at lower altitudes, on the remains of natural vegetation as well as in waste places. Its range, like that of the Phoenix, extends from Europe to North America. The moth is interesting in that it does not hide during the day. It simply sits on a leaf or on a tree trunk and still escapes notice, for its coloration makes it look like bird droppings.

The Yellow Shell (*Camptogramma bilineata* L.) is one of many species (in Europe there are more than 100) that were formerly grouped in a single genus, *Larentia* Tr. Later, this heterogenous group of species was divided into tens of genera (e. g. *Lampropteryx, Ecliptopera, Chloroclysta*). The Yellow Shell is one of the most abundant geometrids and inhabits the entire Palaearctic region.

3

5

The Phoenix (1) has a wingspan of 30—35 mm. There is one generation a year, on the wing from June till August. The eggs hibernate. The caterpillar (2) lives in May and June, feeding on various shrubs and trees of the genus *Prunus*. The pupal stage (3) is very brief.

192

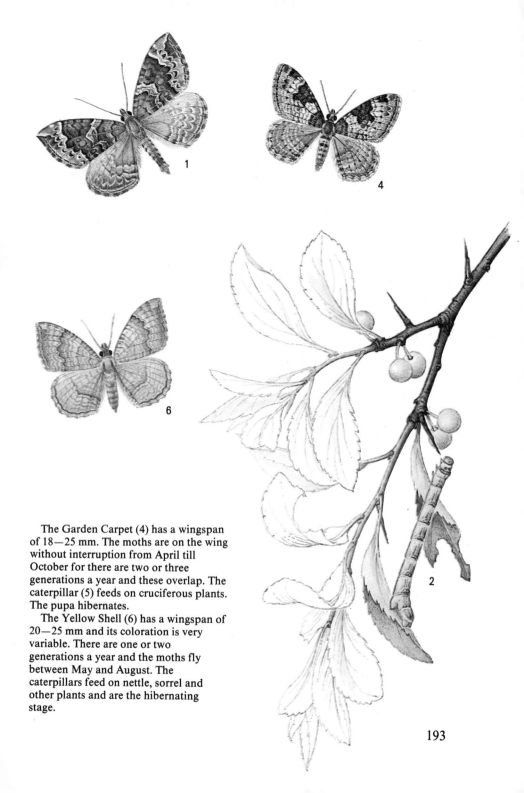

The Garden Carpet (4) has a wingspan of 18—25 mm. The moths are on the wing without interruption from April till October for there are two or three generations a year and these overlap. The caterpillar (5) feeds on cruciferous plants. The pupa hibernates.

The Yellow Shell (6) has a wingspan of 20—25 mm and its coloration is very variable. There are one or two generations a year and the moths fly between May and August. The caterpillars feed on nettle, sorrel and other plants and are the hibernating stage.

193

Magpie
Abraxas grossulariata L.

Some species of animals have figured in history for their economic importance, others by aiding scientific progress. What the white mouse or laboratory 'rat' are to medicine, the Vinegar Fly (*Drosophila melanogaster*) and the Magpie are to genetics. It was while working on these insects that scientists discovered the two basic types of embryonic cells in the animal realm, which were then named after them. A male with the 'Drosophila' embryonic cell produces two types of sperm, differing in the shape of the sex chromosomes, whereas the eggs are of a single kind. A female with the 'Abraxas' cell produces two types of eggs, but the sperm is of one kind. Of the vertebrates, mammals belong to the first type, and birds, for example, to the second.

The Magpie is a forest species of the Palaearctic region exhibiting marked variability in coloration. The caterpillars formerly caused much damage to cultivated Gooseberries and currants. Nowadays this moth has vanished from many localities.

The Brimstone Moth (*Opisthograptis luteolata* L.) is such a unique geometrid with its bright yellow colouring that there is no mistaking it for any other species. It is distributed in Europe and Asia as far as eastern Siberia. It occurs in abundance in forest-steppe areas, on shrubby slopes and in parks and gardens.

5

The Magpie (1) has a wingspan of
35—40 mm. There is one generation
a year. The moths are on the wing in June
and July and sometimes still in August.
The caterpillar (2) develops between
August and the autumn, then hibernates
and completes its development the
following spring. It pupates in a spun-up
leaf (3). Its food plants are Gooseberry,
currant, Blackthorn, hazel etc.

The Brimstone Moth (4) has
a wingspan of 32—37 mm; the female is
larger than the male. There is one
generation a year. The moths are on the
wing from the end of April till July. The
caterpillar (5), which is polyphagous,
lives in August and September on
Hawthorn, Blackthorn, Woodbine,
Bilberry, willow and the like. The pupa
hibernates.

195

Swallow-tailed Moth

Ourapteryx sambucaria L.

The Swallow-tailed Moth is one of the largest species of geometrids. In appearance as well as size it resembles a butterfly, but an expert will recognize at a glance that the type of antennae and the head are those of a moth. Its way of life also differs from that of a butterfly for it is active at night. It lives in the western part of the Palaearctic region; in Asia it has only a scattered, local distribution, and in Europe it is absent from all higher elevations. In the warm lowlands, however, it is a very abundant species. It even seems that its numbers are increasing. This may perhaps be due to the fact that its food plant, the Elder, has likewise become very widespread.

The subfamily Ennominae, which embraces many relatively large, yellow, orange, to brown coloured moths, also includes the Large Thorn (*Ennomos autumnaria* Wernb.). This is an extremely variable moth. It has an enormous range, embracing Europe, Asia and North America, in all parts of which it occurs in broad-leaved forests and forest-steppe areas, chiefly in warmer, lowland districts. It has also developed a liking for fruit orchards and city parks and occurs in large numbers there. An unusual deviation is the dark brown form *schultzi*, whose wings have a violet sheen. There are also differences between the male and female — in the shape of the antennae, in size, and in coloration. The female is larger and is paler and less speckled than the male.

3

The Swallow-tailed Moth (1) has a wingspan of 40—50 mm. There is one generation a year, and the moths are on the wing from June to August. The caterpillars develop between the summer and the following spring, generally pupating in May. They feed on the leaves of Alder, occasionally also Lilac, Blackthorn, Clematis, Aspen, etc.

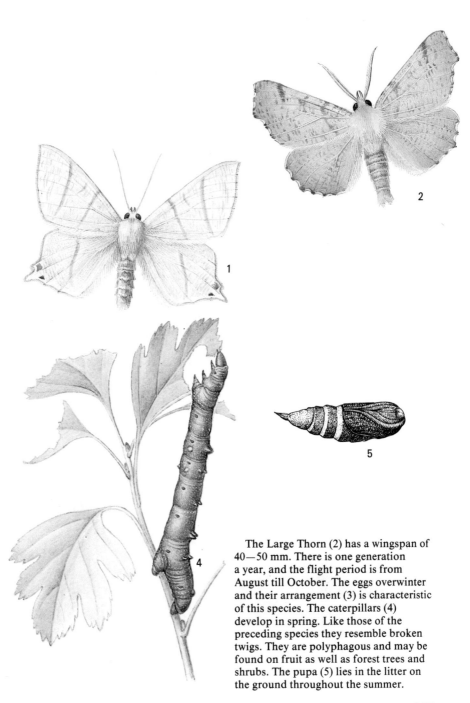

The Large Thorn (2) has a wingspan of 40—50 mm. There is one generation a year, and the flight period is from August till October. The eggs overwinter and their arrangement (3) is characteristic of this species. The caterpillars (4) develop in spring. Like those of the preceding species they resemble broken twigs. They are polyphagous and may be found on fruit as well as forest trees and shrubs. The pupa (5) lies in the litter on the ground throughout the summer.

Peppered Moth
Biston betularia L.

Geometridae

This moth has become very popular of late and has been the subject of many articles in scientific journals. In the nineteenth century a dark mutation (f. *carbonaria*) appeared in the industrial areas of England and this gradually began to supersede the original, typically 'peppered' form. Towards the end of the nineteenth century it began to appear also on the European continent. Nowadays it is the predominating type throughout most of its range. It is believed that the black mutation is somehow connected with the effect of industrial fumes. It is genetically dominant, which means that it prevails in the offspring and apparently has certain advantages, in the cryptic colouring as well as general hardiness, compared with the original type. Research in various European countries has revealed that melanistic forms certainly are an indication of atmospheric pollution. This problem, however, is much more complex than was originally believed, for intermediate forms that are not entirely black (f. *insularia*) have a much more complicated heredity than the entirely black form *carbonaria*. The Peppered Moth is a common inhabitant of the forests of Europe and Asia. There are related species in North America.

The related Oak Beauty (*Biston strataria* Hfn.) has likewise recently begun producing dark coloured forms. It is distributed in the western part of the Palaearctic region and is found in biotopes similar to those frequented by the Peppered Moth.

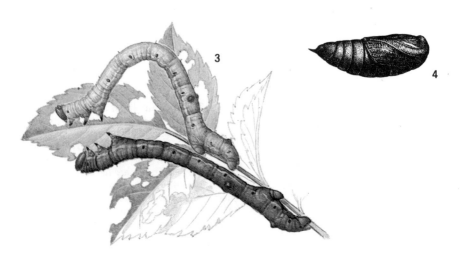

3

4

198

The Peppered Moth has a wingspan of
35—60 mm. The male has comb-like
antennae, while those of the female are
bristle-like. The coloration of the moth is
very variable. The two extreme forms are
the typical 'peppered' form (1) and the
black form (2). There is one brood a year,
and the moths are on the wing from May
till July. The caterpillars (3), which are
polyphagous, are variously coloured.
They feed from June till September on
various shrubs and trees as well as
herbaceous plants such as Lucerne and
Wormwood. The pupa (4) lies in the
ground and hibernates.

The Oak Beauty (5) has a wingspan of
40—50 mm. Moths of the single
generation are on the wing early in
spring, from March till May. The
caterpillar is polyphagous and lives from
May till July. The pupa hibernates.

Large Emerald
Geometra papilionaria L.

Geometridae

Green is definitely an unusual colour for lepidopterans. Only in a few families will one find an occasional green species, for instance amongst the noctuids and tortricids. However, among the geometrids there is an entire subfamily, the Geometrinae, whose members are coloured various shades of green. Some 25 of these are found in Europe. The largest is the Large Emerald, from which the entire family Geometridae derives its name. It inhabits the broad-leaved forest zone in Europe and Asia, its range extending to the Far East — to Kamchatka and Sakhalin. Its favourite haunts are damp, warm, broad-leaved forests with birch, and valley forests with Alder. This moth is not particularly abundant anywhere, but it is found most frequently in the foothills. The pattern on the wings is very variable, nor is the green coloration constant. When the moth emerges from the pupa it is dark green but gradually becomes increasingly lighter. There are difficulties with preserving moths of this colour for collections. Moths must be set immediately after capture, for otherwise straw-coloured spots appear on the wings during the process of relaxing dry specimens and remain permanent.

The most abundant of the inconspicuously-coloured geometrid moths is the Mottled Beauty (*Alcis repandata* L.). Its distribution is similar to that of the preceding species, though it is found in coniferous as well as broad-leaved forests from lowland to mountain regions. It has a tendency towards melanism, for example the entirely black form *nigricata*. Dark forms occur chiefly in industrial areas but their numbers fluctuate from year to year under the influence of the weather.

3

The Large Emerald (1) has a wingspan of 40—50 mm. The male has comb-like (pectinate) antennae, the female thread-like (filiform) antennae. There is one generation a year with the moths on the wing from June till August, depending on the altitude. The caterpillar (2) lives from September, feeding on the leaves of birch, Alder, willow, hazel and other trees. It hibernates and in May of the following year pupates (3) among leaves spun together.

The Mottled Beauty (4) has a wingspan of 30—40 mm. The male has pectinate and the female filiform antennae. The coloration as well as the markings on the wings are very variable. There is one generation a year. The moths are on the wing from May till August in great numbers. The caterpillar hibernates. It lives on broad-leaved as well as coniferous trees.

1

4

2

Cnaemidophorus rhododactyla
Den. et Schiff.

Pterophoridae

Though not very large the family of plume moths is an interesting one. It numbers approximately 600 species worldwide, with more than 100 of them in Europe. These moths generally have the wings divided into two or three plumes resembling bird feathers, and they hold the wings outspread when at rest. They have developed mouthparts. *Cnaemidophorus rhododactyla* is one of the most abundant and colourful species. It is distributed throughout the entire northern hemisphere in rather dry forest-steppe biotopes, on shrubby banks and in pasturelands where the Dog Rose is prevalent. It is also commonly found in agricultural areas not sprayed with chemicals.

Stenoptilia pterodactyla L., with similar distribution, is another abundant species. It is found in thin, broad-leaved forests and forest margins, in forest-steppe areas and in grassy localities. It has a typical cinnamon colour. Like all plume moths it flies only at night, hiding in the vegetation during the day.

Best known is apparently the White Plume Moth (*Pterophorus pentadactyla* L.), which is noted for its snow-white colouring. Except for Spain, it is distributed throughout all of Europe and the temperate regions of Asia — in steppe and forest-steppe areas. In mountains it may be encountered up to an altitude of 1000 m.

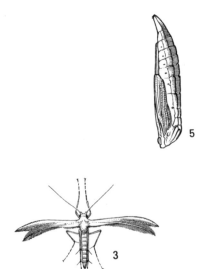

5

Cnaemidophorus rhododactyla (1) has a wingspan of 20—25 mm. There is one generation a year and the moths are on the wing from June till August. The caterpillar lives from September to May; it feeds on the flower buds of the Dog Rose.

Stenoptilia pterodactyla L. (2) has a wingspan of 20—25 mm. When resting, it places the hind wings under the forewings (3). There are two generations a year; the first flies in June and July, the second in August and September. The caterpillar (4) may be seen in July and then again from September till May (it hibernates) on Birdseye Speedwell. It feeds on the top parts of the stem, the buds, the flowers and the unripe ovaries. It pupates on the plant (5).

3

1

2

4

6

The White Plume Moth (6) has
a wingspan of 28—35 mm. There is one
generation a year, on the wing from May
till September. The caterpillar, which is
polyphagous, lives from summer until
May of the following year.

Pyralids are small, or at most medium-sized, moths with broad hind wings. They generally fly at night. There are approximately 20 000 species worldwide, with about 600 of them in Europe. This heterogenous family is divided by some authorities into several smaller families, e. g. Crambidae, Pyraustidae etc.

The subfamily Crambinae forms a distinctive group. One of the most abundant species of this group is *Crambus nemorella* Hb., known in older literature by the synonym *Crambus pratellus* L. It is distributed in both lowland and mountain districts in Europe and Asia. Like the other related species, it has long, forward-directed palps. It is found on grasses.

The Meal Moth (*Pyralis farinalis* L.) feeds on seeds and plant remains in the wild. However, it found superbly suited conditions in mills and flour-product stores and, being shipped with these products to all parts of the globe, now has an almost worldwide distribution.

An interesting group of pyralids are those whose caterpillars feed on aquatic plants. Some species of caterpillars have even become adapted to life in water to such a degree that their breathing organs (tracheae) protrude from the body to form gills with which they absorb oxygen directly from the water. One such abundant species is the Brown China-mark (*Nymphula nymphaeata* L.). This dainty moth lives in the waters of the temperate regions of Europe. The caterpillar is often a pest of water lilies growing in park or garden pools.

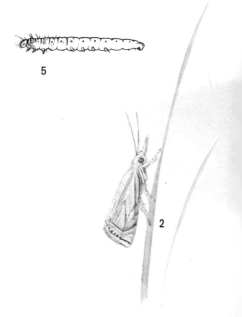

Crambus nemorella Hb. has a wingspan of 19—22 mm. The male (1) is darker than the female (2). The moth rests with wings typically pressed close to the sides of the body. There is one generation a year with moths on the wing between May and July. The caterpillar feeds on various grasses from August till the following spring.

The Meal Moth (3) has a wingspan of 18—30 mm. There is one generation a year, and the moths are on the wing from June till August. The caterpillar, which hibernates, feeds on seeds and plant litter or in flour and flour-product stores. The modern method of storing flour in silos has limited the damage caused by this moth.

5

2

The Brown China-mark (4) has a wingspan of 22—30 mm. The moths of the single generation are on the wing in June and July. The caterpillar (5) lives from August till the following spring on aquatic plants.

Six-spot Burnet
Zygaena filipendulae L.

Zygaenidae

This species is the most abundant of all the members of this family. They are very characteristic moths with black wings patterned with red, yellow or white spots or with greenish forewings with a metallic sheen. There are approximately 1000 species worldwide, 50 of them found in Europe. The Six-spot Burnet is distributed from Europe to central Asia, where it is found in lowlands as well as mountain districts up to heights of 2000 m in grassy places, forest margins and clearings, and on hillsides where there are plenty of flowers rich in nectar. Like the other related species, it is diurnal in habit and on sunny days it visits one flower after another in rather cumbersome flight. It is not wary. Frequently, several moths may be found resting on the large flower of a thistle or Field Scabious in company with bees, bumble bees and other insects.

Zygaena carniolica Sc. is a thermophilous, steppe species. Its distribution is restricted to central and southern Europe, Asia Minor, Iran and the warm parts of Asia to the Altai. In mountains it may be encountered at higher altitudes only in sun-warmed places, mostly on limestone substrates. The coloration of the wings is extremely variable, and there are therefore many forms.

Zygaena ephialtes L., distributed in the temperate zone of Europe and Asia, is also extremely variable. Besides the many individual forms there are also several hereditary varieties, e. g. f. *peucedani* with red markings and f. *icterica* with yellow spots on the wings.

The Six-spot Burnet (1) has a wingspan of 30—38 mm. There is one generation a year, which is on the wing from June till September. The caterpillar (2) lives from autumn until the following June (like other species) on coronilla, Dropwort, clover, Wild Thyme, etc. Before pupating, it spins a glossy yellow cocoon (3) inside which it pupates.

Zygaena carniolica Sc. (4) has a wingspan of 25—32 mm. There is one generation a year, and the moths are on the wing from June till August. The pale green caterpillar feeds on various leguminous plants. The cocoon is oval and whitish.

1

5

3

2

Zygaena ephialtes L. (5) has a wingspan
of 30—40 mm. The moths of the single
generation are on the wing from June till
October. The caterpillars feed on
coronilla, clover and Wild Thyme. The
cocoon containing the pupa is
spindle-shaped and silvery.

There are some 4000 species of Oecophoridae distributed throughout the world, and when we add to them the 5000 species of the Gelechiidae family, formerly placed with them in a single family, this represents one of the largest groups of so-called microlepidopterans. The moths of the Oecophoridae family exhibit great variation in both shape and coloration and likewise have widely differing ways of life. *H. forficella* is one of the larger members of the family. It is found in the broad-leaved forests of Europe and Asia, from lowlands to their upper limit where they give way to natural spruce stands. It prefers damp localities. The caterpillars live under the bark of decaying tree trunks and stumps and are very sensitive to lack of moisture.

A similar range is occupied by the very ornamental species *Oecophora bractella* L. Its yellow and black colouring and greenish white spots with metallic lustre are an unusual combination even in the realm of butterflies and moths. Its attractiveness is even greater when viewed through the microscope, which reveals the long fringe on the edge of the wings.

Diurnea fagella Den. et Schiff. is quite an inconspicuous moth in comparison with the two previous species. The female has vestigial wings and does not fly. This small species exhibits marked variation in coloration, and melanistic forms have begun to appear in great numbers in recent years, particularly in industrial areas. This species is found in forests and orchards from Europe to central Asia, from lowlands to the upper limit of broad-leaved forests.

Harpella forficella (1) has a wingspan of 21—27 mm. There is one generation a year. The moths are in flight in June and July. The caterpillar lives from summer until the following spring. This is an abundant species in damp forests. *Oecophora bractella* (2) has a wingspan of 12—16 mm. There is one generation

2

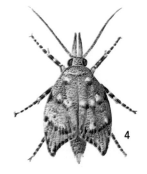

4

a year. The moths are on the wing in
damp forests in May and June at night,
but occasionally also in the daytime. The
development of the caterpillar is the same
as in the preceding species. This is
a relatively rare species.

Diurnea fegalla has a wingspan of
19—29 mm. The males (3) have normal
wings, the females (4) only vestigial
wings. There is one generation a year.
This moth is one of the earliest to appear
in spring, flying at night from March till

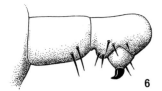

May. The caterpillar (5) is polyphagous
and coloured green. Of interest is the
third pair of legs (6), which it moves
rapidly back and forth when irritated.

Hornet Moth
Sesia apiformis Cl.

There are some 1000 species of clearwings distributed throughout the world, mostly in South America and the tropical regions of the other continents. Only 30 or so are found in Europe. These unusual moths often have wings with translucent, scaleless areas and the black abdomen is frequently marked with yellow or red transverse stripes. In appearance they resemble various aggressive hymenopterous or dipterous insects such as wasps, bees, Sphecidae and robber-flies. However, they are defenceless moths and this likeness to predacious insects is used by them for protection. Their resemblance to various insects is reflected in the Latin names of some species. Clearwings fly during the day. The Hornet Moth is one of the largest European species. It is found in the warmer parts of Europe, central Asia and Siberia and also in North America, living exclusively in lowland localities with various species of poplar.

The Currant Clearwing (*Synanthedon tipuliformis* Cl.) has an almost worldwide distribution (Europe, Asia, North America, Australia, New Zealand). It was introduced to many areas with consignments of currant bushes, for it is a pest of these plants.

Pennisetia hylaeiformis Lasp. is found in Europe, Asia Minor and central Asia practically everywhere that Raspberries grow. The caterpillar may often be seen on Raspberry bushes whereas the moth is seen only rarely. This species occasionally may cause damage in raspberry plantations.

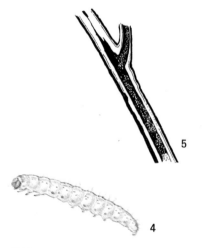

5

4

The Hornet Moth (1) has a wingspan of 30—40 mm. The moths are on the wing during the day between May and August. The caterpillar (2) takes two years to develop, pupating in the spring of the second year after hibernating twice. It bores beneath the bark of poplars on the lower part of the trunk.

The Currant Clearwing (3) has a wingspan of 16—18 mm. Moths of the single generation are on the wing during the day from June till August. The caterpillar (4) develops inside the stems

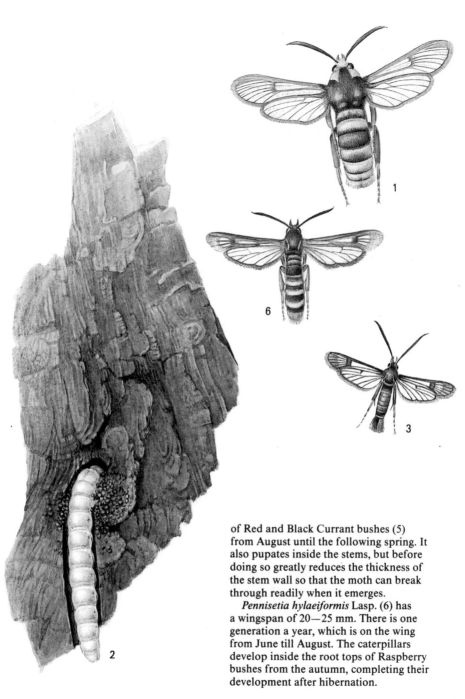

1

6

3

2

of Red and Black Currant bushes (5)
from August until the following spring. It
also pupates inside the stems, but before
doing so greatly reduces the thickness of
the stem wall so that the moth can break
through readily when it emerges.

Pennisetia hylaeiformis Lasp. (6) has
a wingspan of 20—25 mm. There is one
generation a year, which is on the wing
from June till August. The caterpillars
develop inside the root tops of Raspberry
bushes from the autumn, completing their
development after hibernation.

Lilac Leaf Miner
Gracillaria syringella F.

Gracillariidae

The Family Gracillariidae is relatively well represented in Europe. At least 200 species are found there out of the 2000 that are distributed worldwide. These are very small moths with a wingspan of only 6—15 mm. The antennae are practically the same length as the forewings. The caterpillars mine in leaves. The shape of these mines is so characteristic for the individual species that it serves as a means of identification, especially if it is known what plant the given species feeds on. Differentiation of the moths is extremely difficult because they are very much alike; preparation of the copulatory organs is very laborious and requires a microscope. The Lilac Leaf Miner is found only in Europe, in rather warm forests with thick shrubby undergrowth. It also inhabits city parks and gardens. The moth rests on the leaves of shrubs.

The large genus *Phyllonorycter* Hb., embracing a great many species, is generally limited to broad-leaved trees and shrubs. The way of life of the various species is more or less the same: one or two generations a year, with the caterpillars hibernating inside blister-like mines in fallen leaves and pupating there in the spring. The moths emerge shortly after. Best known is *P. blancardella* F., sometimes occurring on apple trees in such numbers that it weakens their growth. Alders in riverine forests are mined by the caterpillar of *P. kleemannella* F., likewise very abundant, and various species of maple by *P. sylvella* Hw.

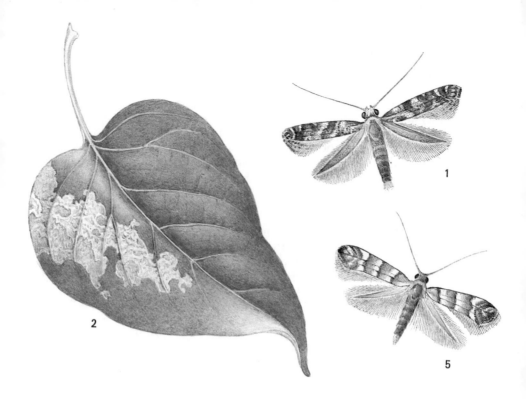

The Lilac Leaf Miner (1) has a wingspan of 12—14 mm. There are two generations a year, the first being on the wing in April and May, the second in August. The caterpillars make blister-like mines (2) in the leaves of Lilac, Privet and ash trees. When fully grown they leave the mines and pupate on the ground. The pupae of the second generation hibernate.

Phyllonorycter blancardella F. (3) has a wingspan of 6—8 mm. There are two generations a year. The moths are on the wing in May and then again in August. The mine (4) is faintly convex on the upper surface of the leaf and membranous on the underside.

Phyllonorycter kleemannella F. (5) has a wingspan of 6—8 mm. It is reported to have one generation a year. The caterpillars live on alders in mines shaped like those of the preceding species.

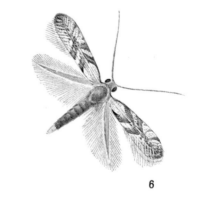

Phyllonorycter sylvella Hw. (6) is the same size and makes the same kind of mines as the two preceding species. It is tied to various species of maple.

Pine-shoot Moth
Rhyacionia buoliana Den. et Schiff.

Tortricidae

Leaf-rollers are small, relatively primitive moths with a wingspan generally less than 20 mm. The current system of classification places them next to phylogenetically very little developed groups of moths. It is estimated that there are more than 5000 species worldwide, most of them distributed in the temperate zone. Some 500 species of leaf rollers are found in Europe. The wings are trapezoidal in shape and close roof-like over the body when the moth is at rest; in some species their coloration is extremely variegated. The moths are active at night.

The Pine-shoot Moth is commonly found in young pine forests. It usually lives on trees that are about 10 years old and damages the shoots. For this reason it is considered a serious pest by foresters. It is distributed throughout the entire northern hemisphere and has been introduced even into South America.

The Green Oak Tortrix (*Tortrix viridana* L.) is occasionally a pest of oaks. The caterpillars may cause complete defoliation of whole forest stands in spring. It is distributed in oak woods from northern Africa through all of Europe and Asia Minor to the Caucasus. It may also cause damage in city parks.

The Marbled Orchard Tortrix (*Hedya nubiferana* Hw.) is a common, colourful little moth with a range similar to that of the preceding species. The caterpillars hatch in spring and can cause widespread damage to the opening buds of fruit trees in orchards.

The species *Olethreutes siderana* Tr. is very ornamental. Its caterpillars live on *Spiraea* in damp biotopes in the temperate and more northerly latitudes of Europe and Asia.

The Pine-shoot Moth (1) has a wingspan of 16—20 mm. The moths of the single generation are on the wing from June till August. The caterpillar (2) causes the malformation and even death of young pine shoots.

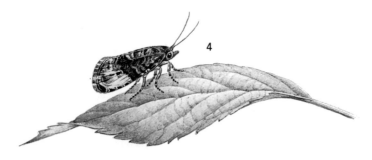

3

The Green Oak Tortrix (3) has a wingspan of 18—23 mm. The moths of the single generation are on the wing in June and July. The eggs hibernate, and the caterpillars live in spring when the oak trees begin growth.

The Marbled Orchard Tortrix (4) has a wingspan of 18—20 mm. There is one generation a year with the moths on the wing in June and July. The eggs hibernate. The caterpillar is polyphagous.

Olethreutes siderana (5) has a wingspan of 16—18 mm. The moths fly in June and July. The eggs hibernate. The caterpillars emerge in spring and feed on *Spiraea*.

5

1

2

Goat Moth
Cossus cossus L.

Cossidae

The goat moths are primitive moths on the evolutionary scale even though some are very large. There are approximately 600 species distributed throughout the world. Most are found in the tropics, less than 10 in Europe. The Goat is one of the large species. It inhabits broad-leaved forests in northern Africa, Europe and Asia to the Far East. In mountains it may be encountered as far as the limit of the broad-leaved forest. However, it generally occurs alongside streams and rivers, if there are trees there, for the caterpillars burrow in the wood of various trees. Such infestation of trees is recognizable at a distance by the smell of wood-vinegar; also, sawdust can be seen falling out of the openings of the gnawed-out galleries. The fully grown caterpillar excavates a roomy chamber in the wood, where it makes a cocoon of sawdust and silken fibres in which it pupates. In spring fully grown caterpillars often abandon the tree in which they lived to pupate on another tree and this is the period when they are most often to be seen. They bite.

The Leopard (*Zeuzera pyrina* L.) is distributed in Europe and Asia and also occurs in North America where it was introduced in the nineteenth century. The caterpillars of this species too bore galleries in wood. The moths vary in size depending on the quality of the food available to the caterpillar. The markings on the wings are very variable. This is an abundant species and is often drawn to light.

3

5

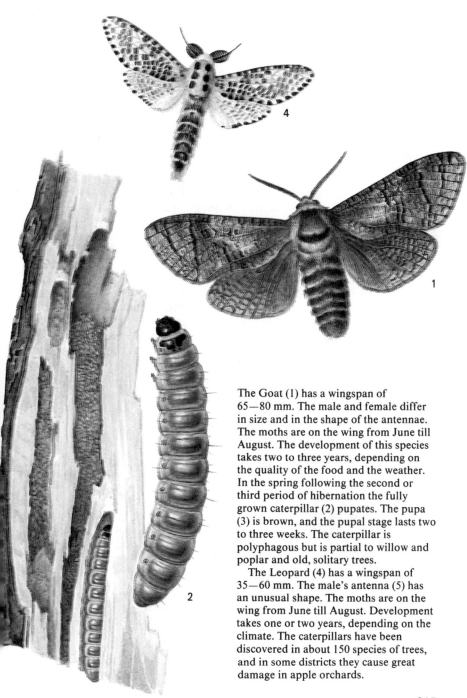

The Goat (1) has a wingspan of
65—80 mm. The male and female differ
in size and in the shape of the antennae.
The moths are on the wing from June till
August. The development of this species
takes two to three years, depending on
the quality of the food and the weather.
In the spring following the second or
third period of hibernation the fully
grown caterpillar (2) pupates. The pupa
(3) is brown, and the pupal stage lasts two
to three weeks. The caterpillar is
polyphagous but is partial to willow and
poplar and old, solitary trees.

The Leopard (4) has a wingspan of
35—60 mm. The male's antenna (5) has
an unusual shape. The moths are on the
wing from June till August. Development
takes one or two years, depending on the
climate. The caterpillars have been
discovered in about 150 species of trees,
and in some districts they cause great
damage in apple orchards.

217

The relatively small family of longhorns numbers about 250 known species worldwide. Approximately 120 species of these are distributed in the Palaearctic region including some 30 that are found in Europe. They are small moths with a wingspan of usually less than 20 mm. However, they have remarkably long antennae, particularly the males. The attractively coloured *Adela degeerella* is one of the common species. It is distributed in broad-leaved and mixed forests throughout the whole of Europe to the Caucasus. On sunny days in damp localities with rich vegetation vast numbers of males may be seen whirling about in clearings and around the twigs of shrubs in a similar fashion to mayflies. As the males fly up and down in a relatively small space, the metallic sheen of their hind wings glitters brightly in the sunlight. The females take no part in these flights but rest somewhere nearby on the leaves of shrubs or herbaceous plants.

In early spring, when Spring Vetchling and *Primula* are in bloom, the small moths of the species *Adela reaumurella* L. may likewise be seen whirling in swarms around the sprouting twigs of maples, oaks, hazels etc. on sunny days. When they alight, their exceedingly long antennae move conspicuously back and forth. This species is distributed in Europe and Asia wherever oak trees grow.

In the mountains one may encounter the less striking species *Nematopogon robertella* Cl. The moths fly singly both during the daytime and at night wherever their food plant, the Bilberry, grows. They are also plentiful in spruce stands up to the upper forest limit.

Adela degeerella has a wingspan of 16—21 mm. The male (1) has long antennae; those of the female (2) are shorter and covered with larger scales. There is one generation a year, on the wing from May till July. The caterpillar mines in leaves at first; later it lives in a case (3). It feeds on Wood Anemone, hibernates, and in spring pupates on the ground.

Adela reaumurella (4) has a wingspan of 14—17 mm. The moths of the single

1

5

4

2

generation are on the wing in April and
May. The caterpillar lives and hibernates
on the ground in a small case and feeds
on dry plant remnants.

Nematopogon robertella (5) has
a wingspan of 12—15 mm. There is one
generation a year. The moths are on the
wing from June till August. The
caterpillar mines in the leaves of the
Bilberry, later living in a small case. It
hibernates.

Ghost Moth
Hepialus humuli L.

Hepialidae

The family of hepialids includes some 400 known species. It is a very old family that has existed on earth for about 200 million years. The first lepidopterans to appear on land looked much like these moths. The very fact that most of the species are found in the Australian region, oasis of archaic types of animals, testifies to the ancient lineage of the hepialids. Only a few, not very large species are found in Europe, but the family includes among its members also the world's largest lepidopterans with a wingspan of more than 20 cm. An archaic characteristic is the similar venation on the forewings and hind wings (in higher lepidopterans the wing venation differs). Among other characteristics are the form of the mouthparts and copulatory organs. The caterpillars feed on plant roots.

The Ghost Moth is distributed in the temperate regions of Europe and Asia to Siberia. It is found from lowlands to mountains but occurs most abundantly in foothill regions. There it flies in damp meadows just before dusk, with the males on the look-out for unfertilized females. Following fertilization the females drop their eggs freely on the grass as they fly.

The cold-loving Gold Swift (*Hepialus hectus* L.) is absent from southern Europe, otherwise it occurs in abundance in central and northern Europe and in Asia, its range extending to the Far East and Sakhalin. It is a woodland species and is on the wing before dusk. In mountains or at the edges of moors where Bilberries grow these moths sometimes occur in whole swarms when the males are busy looking for females.

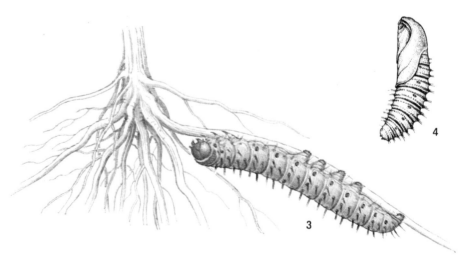

3

4

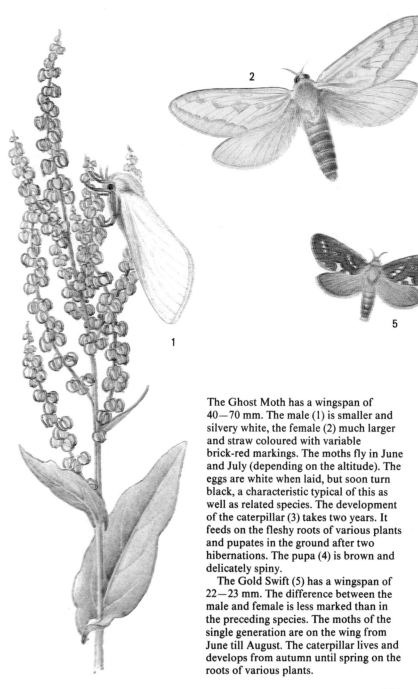

The Ghost Moth has a wingspan of
40—70 mm. The male (1) is smaller and
silvery white, the female (2) much larger
and straw coloured with variable
brick-red markings. The moths fly in June
and July (depending on the altitude). The
eggs are white when laid, but soon turn
black, a characteristic typical of this as
well as related species. The development
of the caterpillar (3) takes two years. It
feeds on the fleshy roots of various plants
and pupates in the ground after two
hibernations. The pupa (4) is brown and
delicately spiny.

The Gold Swift (5) has a wingspan of
22—23 mm. The difference between the
male and female is less marked than in
the preceding species. The moths of the
single generation are on the wing from
June till August. The caterpillar lives and
develops from autumn until spring on the
roots of various plants.

INDEX

Most species references include illustrations.

abdomen 6, 10, 13–14
Abraxas grossulariata 194
Acherontia atropos 166
Acronicta alni 148
  cuspis 148
  menyanthidis 148, 149
  psi 148
  rumicis 148
  tridens 148
adaptation 23
Adela degeerella 218
  reaumurella 218, 219
Admiral, Poplar 48–9, 50
  Red 60
  Southern White 50, 51
  White 50
adult 12–14
Aglais urticae 58
Aglia tau 11, 178
Agrius convolvuli 166
Agrotis exclamationis 140
  ipsilon 141
  segetum 140
Alcis repandata 200
Alder Moth 148
Allancastria cerisii 32
Ammobiota festiva 128–9
Amphipyra berbera 150
  pyramidea 150
  tragopogonis 150
Anthocharis cardamines 38, 39
Apatura ilia 46
  iris 46
Aphantopus hyperantus 94
Apollo 15, 34–5
  Small 34, 35
Aporia crataegi 38
Araschnia levana 17, 62
Arches Moth, Black 136, 137
  Buff 188, 189
Archiearis parthenias 190
Arctia caja 124
  villica 124
Argus, Scotch (Northern Brown) 88
Argynnis paphia 66
Autographa gamma 22, 152

Beauty, Camberwell 56–7
  Mottled 200, 201
  Oak 198, 199
Biston betularia 198
  strataria 198
Blossom, Peach 188–9
Blue, Adonis 116, 117
  Chalk-hill 114–15

Chequered 112, 113
Common 116
Large 110
Silver-studded 112
Small 110, 111
Boloria aquilonaris 70
Brenthis ino 70
Brimstone Butterfly 44–5
Brimstone Moth 194, 195
Brintesia circe 82
Brown, Arran 88, 89
  Dusky Meadow 92, 92–3
  Large Wall 96, 97
  Meadow 92
  Northern, *see* Argus, Scotch
  Northern Wall 96
  Wall 98–9
Brown-tail Moth 24, 38
Buff-tip 162–3
Burnet, Six-spot 206
Burnished Brass Moth 152

Cabbage Moth 144
Callophrys rubi 102
Camptogramma bilineata 192
Carcharodus alceae 118
Carpet Butterfly 192, 193
Carterocephalus palaemon 120
Catocala fraxini 154
  nupta 156
  sponsa 156
caterpillar 8–12, 22, 23, 26–7
Cerura vinula 158
characteristics 6–7, 19
Chataeas graminis 24
Chazara briseis 84
China-mark, Brown 204, 205
Chocolate-tip 162, 163
  Small, 162, 163
Cinnabar Moth 134
classification 17–19
Clearwing, Current 210, 210–11
Clossiana dia 72
  euphrosyne 72
  selene 72
Cnaemidophorus rhododactyla 202
Codling Moth 24
Coenonympha pamphilus 94
Colias australis 40–1
  crocea 40, 40–1
  hyale 40
  palaeno 42
collection 24–6
colouring 6, 12, 15, 16
Comma Butterfly 58, 58–9
Copper, Large 106, 107

Purple-edged 108, 108–9
Scarce 106–7
Small 108
Cossus cossus 216
Crambus nemorella 204
crop spraying effects 27
Cucullia argentea 146
  artemisiae 146
  verbasci 146
Cupido minimus 110
Cycnia mendica 132
Cydia pomonella 24

Dagger, Grey 148, 149
Dasychira pudibunda 138
Deilephila elpenor 172
  porcellus 172
Dendrolimus pini 184
development 7–14
Diachrysia chrysitis 152
diapause 21–2
Diurnea fagella 208, 209
diversity 6, 15–17
dormancy 21
Dot 144, 145
Drinker 180
Dryad 86–7

ecology 19–22
egg(s) 8, 9, 22, 23, 26–7
Eggar, Oak 184
Eilema complana 134
Eligmodonta ziczac 160
Emerald, Large 200
Emperor Butterfly, Greater (Viennese) 176–7
  Lesser Purple 46
  Purple 46
  Tau 11, 178, 179
endangered species 27, 28
Endromis versicolora 186
Ennomos autumnaria 196
environment 6, 20
Ephesia fulminea 154, 155
Erannis defoliara 24
Erebia epiphron 90
  euryale 88
  gorge 90
  ligea 88
  pandrose 90
Ermine, Buff 132
  White 132
Eulithis prunata 192
Euphydryas aurinia 78
  maturna 78
Euplagia quadripunctaria 126
Euproctis chrysorrhoea 24
eyes 12

Fabriciana adippe 68
  niobe 68